The Metaphor of Marriage between YHWH and Israel

YHWH, THE HUSBAND OF ISRAEL

SEOCK-TAE SOHN

Wipf and Stock Publishers
EUGENE, OREGON

Wipf and Stock Publishers
199 West 8th Avenue, Suite 3
Eugene, Oregon 97401

YHWH, The Husband of Israel
By Seock-Tae Sohn
©2002 Seock-Tae Sohn
ISBN: 1-57910-867-9
Publication Date: November, 2002

Preface

The basic idea for this book came from my first book, *The Divine Election of Israel* published by Eerdmans. This book was a reworked version of my doctoral dissertation submitted to the Graduate School of Arts and Science, New York University. As I have taught and worked at Reformed Theological Seminary in Korea, the theme of the marriage metaphor has remained active in my thoughts and has continued to push me to write it down.

Fortunately, Tyndale House of Cambridge provided me an ideal setting to begin writing this book during the period of my sabbatical semester in 1995. However, I could not continue writing when I came back from England because I had to be involved in so many administrative works of my institution. Thus I decided to write the Korean version first and it was published in 1997. It took me almost three years to finish the remaining parts of English version after the publication of Korean version. The theory of metaphor was included in the Korean version. But I omitted it in English version, because it does not give practical help to the readers.

I express my deep gratitude to my students and alumni of Reformed Theological Seminary who patiently sat in the class to listen to my lectures. I also appreciate the favorable encouragements and helpful advices of my dear colleagues in the seminary: professors, Yong-Hwa Na, Kwang-Chae Kim, Kyu-Hyun Chae. I am greatly indebted to Mrs. Sarah Koh who lives in the Holy Land and polished my poor English. Professors Baruch A. Levine of New York University and Tremper Longman, III of Westmont College who have been my teachers from the days of theological education until now deserve to be mentioned their names here. My last and deepest gratitude should be given to Hee-Sook Koh, my wife since she is always good to me.

                                            Seock-Tae Sohn
                                            Reformed Theological Seminary
                                            Seoul, Korea

Contents

Preface	i
Contents	iii
Abbreviations	vii
Introduction	1
CHAPTER I The Marriage Terms	**5**
1. *Lāqaḥ* (לקח, to take)	5
2. *Baʿal* (בעל, to marry)	8
3. *Naśʾ* (נשא, to bring)	12
4. *Hošîḇ* (השיב, to marry, to settle)	14
5. *Hayā leʾišā* (היה לאשה, to be a wife)	16
6. *ʾāraś* (ארש, to engage)	17
7. *Yāḏaʿ* (ידע, to know, to have sexual relation)	18
8. *Pāraś kanap* (פרש כנף, to spread the skirt)	20
9. The Other Terms	21
CHAPTER II The Marriage Formulae	**23**
1. The Declarative Formulae	23
2. The Descriptive Formulae	27
CHAPTER III The Marriage in Israel	**35**
1. The Engagement in Israel	35
2. The Marriage in Israel	37
3. The Marriage Life in Israel	39
4. The Divorce in Israel	40
5. The Remarriage in Israel	41

CHAPTER IV The Marriage between YHWH and Israel	43
1. YHWH's Engagement to Israel	43
2. YHWH's Marriage to Israel	45
3. YHWH's Dwelling among Israel	50
4. YHWH's Divorce from Israel	54
5. YHWH's Remarriage to Israel	62
CHAPTER V The Marriage Texts	67
1. The Book of Hosea 1-3	67
(1) Hosea and his time (1:1)	68
(2) Hosea and Gomer (1:2-9)	70
(3) YHWH and Israel (1:10-2:23)	74
(4) YHWH and Hosea (3:1-5)	82
2. The Book of Jeremiah	84
(1) Jeremiah 2:1-37	85
(2) Jeremiah 3:1-18	86
(3) Jeremiah 31:31-34	94
3. The Book of Ezekiel	97
A. Ezekiel 16	97
(1) The Birth of Jerusalem (1-5)	97
(2) The Marriage of Jerusalem (6-14)	99
(3) The Adultery of Jerusalem (15-34)	102
(4) The Judgment of Jerusalem (35-59)	108
(5) The Restoration of Jerusalem (60-63)	114
B. Ezekiel 23	117
(1) The Harlotry of Oholah and Oholibah(1-4)	117
(2) The Harlotry and Punishment of Oholah (5-10)	118

Contents

    (3) The Harlotry and Punishment of Oholibah(11-35)   120
    (4) The Punishment of Oholah and Oholibah (36-49)   126

4. Other Texts   128

CHAPTER VI Christ and the Church as a Husband and Wife   133

    1. The Johannine Literature   134
    2. The Synoptic Gospels   136
    3. The Pauline Epistles   137
        (1) 2Cor. 11:1-3   137
        (2) Eph. 5:21-33   138

Conclusion   141
Bibliography   145
Name Index   151
Scripture Index   153

Abbreviations

AASOR	*Annual of the American School of Oriental Research*
AB	The Anchor Bible
Ahw	*Akkadisches Handwörterbuch.* W. von Soden, 3 vols. Wiesbaden, 1965-81.
ANET	*Ancient Near Eastern Texts.* Edited by J. B. Prichard. 3rd ed. Princeton, 1969.
BAP	Maiguer, *Beiträge zum altbabylonischen Privatrecht.* Leipzig: Hinrichs, 1893.
BASOR	*Bulletin of the American Schools of Oriental Research*
BDB	*The New Brown-Driver-Briggs-Gesenius Hebrew-Aramaic Lexicon.* Peabody: Hedrickson, 1979.
BHS	*Biblia Hebraica Stuttgartensia,* ed. K. Elliger and W. Rudolph (1983)
BIN	*Babylonian Inscriptions in the Collection of J. B. Nies*; 8 vols; vol. 2 =J. B. Nies and C. E. Keiser, *Historical, Religious and Economic Texts and Antiquities* (New Haven :Yale, 1920); vol. 7= J. B. Alexander, Early Babylonian Letters and Economic Texts (New Haven: Yale, 1943).
BMAP	E.G. Kraeling, *Brooklyn Museum Aramaic Papyri.* New Haven: Yale University Press, 1953.
CAD	*The Assyrian Dictionary of the Oriental Institute of the University of Chicago.*
CBC	The Cambridge Bible Commentary
CBQ	*The Catholic Biblical Quarterly*
CH	Code of Hammurabi
CT	*Cuneiform Texts from Babylonian Tablets, etc., in the British Museum,* 52 vols. (1896-).
CTA	A. Herdner, *Corpus des Tablettes en cunéiformes alphabéiques DISO.* C. F. Jean-J. Hoftijzer, *Dictionnaire des Inscriptions*

	Sémitiques de l'Quest, Leiden 1965.
DISO	*Dictionnaire des inscriptions sémitiques de l'oust.* edited by Ch. Jean and Hoftijzer, Leiden, 1965
DOTT	*Documents from Old Testament Times,* Edited by W.W. Thomas, London,1958.
EEC	*An Exegetical and Expoisitory Commentary, The Minor Prophets.* vol.1. ed.by Thomas Edward McComskey, Grand Rapids: Baker, 1992.
HAL	Koehler, L., W. Baumgartner and J.J. Stamm. *Hebräisches und Aramäisches Lexikon zum Alten Testament.* Fascicles 1-5. 1967- 1995 (KBL 3). ET: HACOT
HSS	*Harvard Semetic Studies,* 24 vols.
HTR	*Harvard Theological Review*
JAOS	*Journal of the American Oriental Society*
JBL	*Journal of Biblical Literature*
JNES	*Jouranl of Near Eastern Studies*
JNSL	*Journal of Northwest Semitic Languages*
JSOT	*Journal for the Study of Old Testament*
JSRT	*Jouranl for the Study of Reformed Theology*
Kich	*Excavations at Kish, S. Langdon(Paris, 1924-34)*
MAL	*Middle Assyrian Laws*
MRS	Mission de Ras Shamra
MT	Masoretic Text
NASB	New American Standard Bible
NCC	The New Century Commentary
NKJV	New King Jamed Version
NICNT	*New International Commentary on the New Testament*
NICOT	*New International Commentary on the Old Testament*
NIV	New International Version
NKJV	New King James Version
OTL	The Old Testament Library
PBS	*Publications of the Babylonians Section* (Philadelphia:University Museum, University of Pennsylvania). 8/2 Edward Chiera, Old Babylonian Contracts. 1922
PEFQS	Palestine Exploration Fund Quarterly Statement
POT	De Prediking van net Oude Testament. eds. A. van Selms, A.S. van der Woude, and C. van Leeuween. Nijkerk: G.F. Callenbach, 1984.

Abbreviation

PRU	*Le Palais Royal d'Ugarit*, ed. C. F. A. Schaffer- J. Nougayrol, Paris
RS	Ras Shamra
TDNT	*Theological Dictionary of the New Testament.* Edited by G. Kittel and G. Friedrich. Translated by G. W. Bromiley. 10 vols. Grand Rapids. 1964-1976
TDOT	*Theological Dictionary of the Old Testament.* Edited by G. J. Botterweck and H. Riggren. Translated by J. T. Wills, G.W. Bromiley, and D. E. Green. 8 vols. Grand Rapids 1974- Theologia
TNTC	Tyndale New Testament Commentaries
TOTC	Tyndale Old Testament Commentaries
TWAT	*Theologisches Wörterbuch zum Alten Testament.* Edited by G. J. Botterweck and H. Riggren. Stuttgart, 1970-
TIM	A. Al-Zeebari, *Texts in the Iraq Museum* (1964)
UT	*Ugaritic Tesxtbook.* C.H. Gordon. AnOr 38. Rome, 1965
VT	*Vetus Testamentum*
WBC	Word Biblical Commentary
YOS	*Yale Oriental Series.* 12 vols. New Haven: Yale, 1915-1978.

Introduction

The people of Israel believed that they had a special relationship with their God, YHWH. They tried to understand and explain the nature of this relationship through the metaphor of marriage. They even tried to interpret their history in terms of this theme and to foresee their future history through this. Needless to say, the major themes such as election, covenant, rejection and restoration found in the Old Testament are some of the ways used to explain the relationship. What draws our attention here is how Israel described and explained the relationship, something which is not visible, but an untouchable abstract concept. Wisely enough, they employed the use of metaphor in order to illustrate and define this concept.

The metaphor of marriage is one of the typical means used to portray the relationship between YHWH and Israel in the Old Testament along with the metaphors of father-son, shepherd-sheep, king-royal servants, general-soldier, master-slave, farmer-vineyard, etc.[1] In the New Testament not only does Jesus use this metaphor in order to proclaim himself as God as well as the Messiah promised in the Old Testament, but also many of the biblical writers use the same metaphor to explain the relationship between Christ and his church.

In order to understand the metaphor of marriage correctly, a comprehensive knowledge of the concept and practice of marriage in Israel is required. The terms used for marriage and its customs and the concept and meaning implied in the language and related practice are particularly important. In addition, an understanding of the legal responsibilities and obligations attendant to marriage and the ramifications of the collapse of a

---

1. Seock-Tae Sohn, *The Divine Election of Israel* (Grand Rapids: Eerdmans, 1991), 263-65.

marriage due to the unfaithfulness of either spouse and the remarriage of the divorced couple, etc. is indispensable.

Marriage has been the same in nature throughout the world in history. However, it is different from nation to nation in its understanding and expression. For a long period of history Israel communicated the language and culture with their surrounding Semitic nations. They used the same Semitic language and shared a similar culture and customs. However, they maintained a uniqueness which could not be found among their neighbors. This uniqueness calls for a study of the ancient Semitic terms and customs of marriage in order to have a better understanding of the Israelite marriage. In particular, the ancient Semitic languages provide the basic insight for the meaning of marriage. Accordingly, it will be one of the important tasks to examine the ancient Near Eastern practices of marriage.

The metaphor of marriage seems to have been used for a long period of Israelite history, for as long as they worshiped and served YHWH. It might have been used in their ordinary life. However, as their knowledge of YHWH expanded and deepened, their use of the metaphor also developed and was enriched. Conversely, it could be that as their knowledge and meaning of marriage expanded and matured, not only did their knowledge of the metaphor itself grow, but also that of YHWH broadened and deepened. Therefore, the books written in the later period contain more developed and well plotted forms of metaphor, which are more theologically polished and enriched. The major theological themes representing the relationship between YHWH and Israel such as election, covenant, rejection, and restoration are compared and described in terms of engagement, marriage, divorce, and remarriage between man and woman.

As we proceed the discussion on this theme, first of all we will browse the terms for marriage in the Old Testament and its usage. This will lead us to find the etimological meaning of marraige. If necessary, the cognate study of ancient Near Eastern languages will also be traced.

The next step is to find how those marriage terms express the relationship between YHWH and Israel. Since the declarative formulae that are supposed to have used in wedding are very similar to that of covenant formula between YHWH and Israel, the investigaion of the similarlity between the formuae

Introduction

will be of great help to understand the metaphor of marriage.

Following those analysis, the exegesis and interpretation for the selected texts of marriage will show how the concept of human marriage is utilized for theological description and how it is developed as metaphor itself.

Finally, our discussion will be extended to the New Testament. We will trace how the theme of marriage between YHWH and Israel continued and developed in it. In particular, how Jesus employed and used the relationship metaphor of the Old Testament in order to proclaim his divinity and define his relationship with his dischiples will be traced.

CHAPTER I

The Marriage Terms

If metaphor can be said to have arisen from semantic collision and semantic development, the same is true for the marriage metaphor. Many marriage terms are employed to describe the relationship between YHWH and Israel. This requires an investigation of the semantics of marriage terms.

Various expressions are found in the Old Testament to denote the idea of "to marry." Terms such as *lāqaḥ* (לקח), *bāʿal* (בעל), *nāśāʾ* (נשא), *ʾaraṣ* (ארץ), *hāyā lᵉʾišah* (היה לאשה) are frequently used for marriage in the Scriptures. In rare instances, *ḥatan* (חתן) and *yabam* (יבם) are also used. In addition to these, the term *yadaʿ* (ידע), describing physical relations between a husband and his wife, is also important in understanding the concept of marriage. These words will each be examined to determine how they came to carry the meaning of marriage and how they describe the relationship between YHWH and Israel.

1. *Lāqaḥ* (לקח, *to take*)

It is not easy to exactly define the word *lāqaḥ* (לקח) since it is used differently in broad and various contexts. Hebrew dictionaries propose that the root meaning of the word is "to take."[1] A man usually *lāqaḥ* (לקח) something for his possession. From this, the word is in many cases translated

---

1. *BDB*, 542. Gesenius, 441, *HAL*, 507, etc.

as "to have for oneself," or "to possess for oneself."

This word basically carries the concept of possession. In this instance, *lāqaḥ* (לקח) is constructed with a special syntax. It takes the preposition, *lamed* (ל) twice. The first *lamed* (ל) introduces the "taker" or "the direction" of transferring the possession, and it takes as its object the pronoun of the subject, such as *lî* (לי), *lô* (לו), *lahem* (להם) etc. The second *lamed* (ל) represents the usage of the possession.

> The wife of a man from the company of the prophets cried out to Elisha, "Your servant my husband is dead, and you know that he received YHWH. But now his creditor is coming to take my two sons as slaves" (והנשה בא לקחת את־שני ילדי לו לעבדים). (2 Kgs 4:1)

Here, the Hebrew verb *lāqaḥ* (לקח) takes two words introduced by the inseparable preposition, *lamed* (ל). The first word *lô* (לו) signifies the direction of transference of possession from her mother to the creditor. The second word, *laʿabadim* (לעבדים) represents the usage of the creditor's taking of the children for servants. As has been observed here, the usage of *lāqaḥ* (לקח) is very unusual.

In particular, *lāqaḥ* (לקח) is used in the Bible as a marriage term denoting "to marry," or "to take someone as a wife" and as an adoption term carrying the meaning of "to adopt." When *lāqaḥ* (לקח) is used as a marriage term, it represents the concept of a man's possession of a woman or the relationship between a man and a woman as a subject and object in the sentence. In this case as well, *lāqaḥ* (לקח) takes *lamed* (ל) twice and constructs a very special syntax, the marriage formula.

> Amram married his father's sister Jochebed . . .
> (ויקח עמרם את־איוכבד דרתו לו לאשה . . .). (Ex. 6:20)

Here the subject Amram took (*lāqaḥ*, לקח) Jochebed for himself (לו) and for a wife (לאשה). Amram's purpose in taking Jochebed was for her to be his wife. This shows that *lāqaḥ* (לקח) is a marriage term. It is used for a man who takes a woman for his wife.

The Semitic cognates of the Hebrew word *lāqaḥ* (לקח) are also used as marriage terms. The Akkadian cognate of the Hebrew *lāqaḥ* (לקח) is *leqû*. This word also denotes the idea of "to take a wife," or "to adopt."[2] The Ugaritic cognate *lqḥ* also carries the same meaning and is used as a marriage term.[3]

The selection of the spouse in the Hebrew Bible is usually decided by the parents of both the bride and bridegroom. In rare cases, a young man and woman fell in love with each other and got married. Occasionally a man captured a woman on the battle field and took her as a wife (Deut. 20:13-14; Judg. 21:19-24). Usually the man took the initiative in the process of marriage. The marriage term *lāqaḥ* (לקח) carries the meaning of possession, particularly the meaning of a man taking his wife as his possession or property.

At this point the usage of the verb *lāqaḥ* (לקח) draws our special attention. It is not only used as a marriage term, but also as a theological term

---

2. *HAL*. 507.

   RN ma at RN2 ana DAM-ut-ti-s il-te-qé
   Ammistamru took the daughter of Benteŝna as his wife.
   (*CAD*, L. 9:137; MRS 9 126; RS 17.156:6)

3. (203) *hm. ḥry. bty* (204) *iqḥ*
   aš rb. g lmt (205) *ḥrz*
   ṯnh. wspm (206) *atn.*
   w. ṯlṯh. ḥrṣm.

   If I may take Huray (into) my house
   introduce the lass to my court,
   I will give twice her (weight) in silver
   and thrice her (weight) in gold. (*CTA* 14:203-206)

J. C. L. Gibson suggests that *iqḥ* is used with the same meaning as לקח in Gen. 24:67 and Ruth 4:11, 13 (*Canaanite Myths and Legends* [Edinburgh: T. & T. Clark, 1978], 87-88). The same usage is also found in *CTA* 23:35-36.

   (21) *a [tt. tq]ḥ ykrt*
   att (22) *tqḥ btk*
   glmt tš rb (23) *ḥqrk*
   tld š bnm lk

   The [wife whom you] take O! Keret
   The wife whom you take (into) your house,
   the lass whom introduce to your court,
   shall bear you seven sons. (*CTA* 15. col. ii.21)

YHWH, THE HUSBAND OF ISRAEL

describing the relationship between YHWH and Israel.

> I will take you as my own people (לקחתי אתכם לי לעם) and I will be your God. Then you will know that I am YHWH your God, who brought you out from under the yoke of the Egyptians. (Ex. 6:7)

Here we can see that the verb *lāqaḥ* (לקח) takes the preposition *lamed* (ל) twice and is used to establish the relationship between YHWH and Israel. As the first step in establishing the special relationship whereby Israel became the people of YHWH and YHWH became the God of Israel, the verb *lāqaḥ* (לקח) is used.[4] In this case *lāqaḥ* (לקח) is used as an election term.[5] The use of this term as an election term can be seen more clearly in Deut. 4:34.

> Has any god ever tried to take for himself one nation out of another nation (אלהים ... לקחת לו גוי מקרב גוי), by testings, by miraculous signs and wonders, by war, by a mighty hand and an outstretched arm, or by great and awesome deeds, like all the things YHWH your God did for you in Egypt before your very eyes? (Deut. 4:34).

The phrase, "to take for himself one nation out of another nation" (לקחת לו גוי מקרב גוי) obviously implies the concept of election. The marriage term, *lāqaḥ* (לקח) is now used as a theological term of election. [6] *Lāqaḥ* (לקח) is one of the typical election terms. The Biblical writers describe the concept of YHWH's taking of Israel as his people in marital terms of a man taking a woman as his wife. *Lāqaḥ* (לקח) is not only used for YHWH's election of Israel as his people, but also for the election of an individual.

> On that day, declares YHWH Almighty, "I will take you (אקחך) my servant Zerubbabel son of Shealtiel," declares YHWH, "and I will make you like my signet ring, for I have chosen you (כי־בך בחרתי)"declares YHWH Almighty. (Hag. 2:23)

Here the subject of the verbs "to take" and "to choose" is YHWH, and the

---

4. R. E. Clement asserts that this phrase describes the intimate relationship between God and his people and God requires his people to worship him only. *Exodus* (CBC; Cambridge: Cambridge University Press, 1972), 38.
5. Seock-Tae Sohn, *The Divine Election of Israel* (Grand Rapids: Eerdmans, 1991), 15.
6. Ibid., 11-16.

object is Zerubbabel, the individual. It is noteworthy that the verb *lāqaḥ* (לקח) is used as an election term such as *baḥar* (בחר).

2. Ba‛al (בעל, to marry)

The marriage term *ba‛al* (בעל) gives the basic key to understanding the nature of the relationship between a husband and wife. The term *ba‛al* (בעל) as a noun carries the meaning of "owner" or "possessor." In the Hebrew Bible we can find the following phrases: "the owner of the bull" (בעל השור, Ex. 21: 28), "the owner of the pit" (בעל הבור, Ex. 21:34), "the owner of the house" (בעל הבית, Ex. 22:7; Judg. 19:22, 23). The Semitic cognates: *bēlu* (Akkadian), *b‛l* (Ugaritic), and *ba‛la᾿* (Aramaic) also carry the same meaning. If *ba‛al* (בעל) follows *išā* (אשה), or *ha(hen)* (ה[ן]), the feminine pronominal suffix, its meaning is "her master," i.e. " her husband."

Ba‛al (בעל) as a verb carries the meaning "to rule over," or "to possess," but in many cases its meaning is "to marry."

> As a young man marries(יבעל) a maiden,
> so will your sons marry you(יבעלוך);
> as a bridegroom rejoices over his bride
> so will your God rejoice over you. (Isa. 62:5; Cf. Deut. 24:1; Proverb 30:23)

As the usage of the verb *ba‛al* (בעל) shows, marriage implies that the husband is the owner of the girl he has taken and that the wife is the possession of her husband. Through marriage a husband becomes the master, ruler, and owner of his wife.[7] The Ten Commandments classify a wife in the category of a husband's possessions such as a male servant, female servant, ox, and donkey (Ex. 20:17).[8] However, Burrows points out that a wife is not the same type of possession as servants or animals even though *ba‛al* (בעל)

---

7. R. de Vaux, *Ancient Israel*, 2 vols (New York: McGraw-Hill, repr. 1965), 1:26. See also *PRU*. II. No.77; *DISO*, 40 under 2c; Gen. 20:3; 21:3,22; Deut. 22:22; 24:4, etc. *TDOT*. II. 182.
8. Ibid., 39.

carries the double meaning of "possessor" and "husband."⁹ The owner of a servant could sell or even kill the servant, but he could not sell or kill his wife. He could only divorce his wife if she did not fulfill her obligations as a wife. In this case he must follow the legal procedures for securing a divorce. However, a wife could not ask for a divorce from her husband. Furthermore, a wife did not inherit her husband's property.¹⁰ Thus, a wife was never merely a possession; rather, she was a special possession, special property, of her husband. A wife's status in the family was very peculiar.

The Hebrew verb *qanā* (קנה) draws special attention to the nature of the Israelite marriage in terms of marriage as a man's possession of a woman. In Ruth 4:10, Boaz said, "I have also acquired Ruth, the Moabitess, Mahlon's widow, as my wife . . ." (וגם את־רות המאביה אשת מחלון קניתי לי לאשה). The use of the verb *qanā* (קנה) here seems to suggest that the custom of marriage by purchase was practiced at that time. This also seems to prove the concept of marriage as man's possession of a woman. ¹¹

The marriage proclamation also draws our attention in relation to this concept of possession. Usually a husband would proclaim the establishment of his marital relation with his wife at his wedding. One of the typical marriage proclamations is "She is my wife and I am her husband" (ואנכי אשה היא אשתי, or ואנכי בעלה הוא אשתי), or "She is my wife and I am her husband from this day forth and forever" (הי אנתי ואנה בעלה מן יומא זנה ועד עלם).¹² Here the groom calls himself *baʿalā* (בעלה), which means her owner. It should be noted here that the husband does not proclaim to his wife, "I am your husband and you are my wife," but to a third person, "She is my wife and I am her husband." This obviously points to the emphasis on his

---

9. Miller Burrows, "The Ancient Oriental Background of Hebrew Levirate Marriage," *BASOR* 76 (Dec., 1939): 8. *The Basis of Israelite Marriage* (New Heaven: American Oriental Society, 1938), 52-72.

10. Baruch A. Levine, "In Praise of the Israelite *Mišpaḥā* : Legal Themes in the Book of Ruth," in *The Quest of the Kingdom of God: Studies in Honor of George E. Mendenhall*, ed. H. B. Huffmon et al. (Winona Lake: Eisenbrauns, 1983), 103.

11. L. Ginsberg and J. N. Epstein examined that the usage of *qānā* (קנה) and *qādaš* (קדש) substentiated the presence of the practice of marriage by purchase in biblical times as well in post-biblical times. J. N. Epstein, *Prolegomena Ad Litteras Tanniticus* (Hebrew), 1957, 53, 414. David Halivini Weis, "The Use of קנה in connection with Marriage," *HTR* 57 (1957): 244-48.

The Marriage Terms

ownership of the woman, rather than the marriage relationship with her. Therefore, this proves that the concept of ownership in marriage entails a legally binding force. In this respect marriage was a kind of legal contract which required witnesses.

Not only in Israel, but also in the ancient Near East or Canaan is the concept of ownership in marriage found. In an Akkadian context, when Ereshkigal was threatened by Nergal, she pleaded for her life and said:

> You are my husband, I will by thy wife . . .
> Be thou master, I will be thy mistress.
> *(Attā lū muti ma anāku lū aššatka . . .*
> *Attā lū anāku lū bēltu.)* [13]

Here the terms of husband-wife and master-mistress constitute parallelism, and the latter expands and complements the meaning of the former. In an Ugaritic text, there is a list of men classified according to their possession of either a wife or a concubine. In it a man who accompanies a wife is called "a possessor of a wife" (*b'l aṯt*) and a concubine, "a possessor of a concubine" (*b'l ššlmt*).[14]

The Hebrew verb *ba'al* (בעל) is to be noted since it is also used for describing the relationship between YHWH and Israel.

> "In that day," declares the Lord,
> "you will call me 'my husband' (אישי);
> you will no longer call me 'my master' (בעלי)." (Hos. 2:16)

"My husband" could be rendered in Hebrew as either *'îšî* (אישי) or *ba'alî* (בעלי). Here YHWH wants his people to call him *'îšî* (אישי), not *ba'alî*

---

12. This is a marriage proclamation used in the Jewish Aramaic marriage contract found from Elephantine. Mordecai A. Friedman, "Israel's Response in 2:17b: 'You Are My Husband,'" *JBL* 99/2 (1980): 199-200.

13. EA 375:82-85. cf. Gilgamesh Epic Vi 7-9; S. Greengus, "Babylonian Marriage Contract," *JAOS* 89.3 (1969): 516.

14. Cyrus H. Gordon, *Ugaritic Texts* (Rome: Pontifical Biblical Institute, 1965), Text 10777:2-10, 22.

YHWH, THE HUSBAND OF ISRAEL

(בעלי) because *baʿalî* (בעלי) is a homonym representing both husband and Baal, the gods of Canaan. If anyone is called *baʿalî* (בעלי), it could be interpreted as either "my husband," or "my gods, Baal." In Jer. 31: 32 YHWH says that he was a husband to Israel (בעלתי בה) when he made the covenant at Sinai. Thus, *baʿal* (בעל) is one of the important terms used to describe the YHWH-Israel relationship in terms of the marriage concept.

3. *Nāśʾ a* (נשא, *to bring*)

The lexical meaning of *nāśʾa* (נשא) is "to take away," or "to carry away." Sometimes it carries the meaning of "to bring" (2 Kgs 14: 20). When it is used as a marriage term, its meaning is same as that of *lāqaḥ* (לקח).

> They married (acn) Moabite women, one named Orpah and the other Ruth. (Ruth 1:4) [15]

This usage shows that marriage means that a man brings a woman to his house. In a marriage the husband was to bring his wife from her father's house to his. Either the husband himself went to bring the woman for his wife (Ex. 2:1), or sent he another man to bring her to his house (Ex. 24:1; Judg. 14:3; 1Sam. 25:25-39; 2Sam. 11:27).

> After the time of mourning was over, David had her brought to his house (וישלח דוד ויאספה אל־ביתו) and she became his wife and bore him a son. But the thing David did displeased the Lord. (2 Sam. 11:27).

Here *ʾāsap* (אסף) is used instead of *nāśʾa* (נשא) for the meaning of "to bring." Though the primary meaning of *ʾāsap* (אסף) is "to gather," it is used to denote the meaning of to "take in (a wife into a house)" as in this case. It is to be noted here that *šālaḥ* (שלח) and *bôʾ* (בוא) are used together in the marriage context since someone had to go to the house of the bride to bring her to his home. We can find this type of custom in Ugaritic literature. One of

---

15. Gen. 45:27; 46:5; 50:13; 1Sam. 10:3; 18:12; 2Kgs. 4:20; Isa. 40: 11, 24; 41:16; 57:13; Hos. 1:6; 5:14; 2Ch. 10:12.

The Marriage Terms

the most important procedures in an Ugaritic marriage is the bride's entering into the house of her groom. Usually the bride was handed over to her bridegroom by her company, who was waiting for her outside the gate to lead her into his house.[16] The concept of a woman's entering into the house of a man is also found in the Canaanite and Egyptian literatures.[17]

> Has any god ever tried to take for himself one nation out of another nation (או הנסה אלהים לבוא לקחת לו גוי), by testings, by miraculous signs and wonders, by war, by mighty and an outstretched arm, or by great and awesome deeds, like all the things YHWH your God did for you in Egypt before your very eyes? (Deut. 4:34)

The NIV translation omits *labôʾ* (לבוא) here. "Has any god ever tried to go and take . . . " would be closer to the Hebrew text.[18] However, the NIV maintains the correct meaning. YHWH went (לבוא) to Egypt to take (לקח) Israel for his people. It is our assumption that "to go" (בוא) and "to take" (לקח) are intentionally employed together here, since the verb *labôʾ* (לבוא) is not necessary here. Why did God go to Egypt? The answer was to take Israel as his people just as a man went to a woman's house to take her as his wife and bring her to his home.

> I will take (לקחתי) you as my own people, and I will be your God. Then you will know that I am YHWH your God, who brought you out from under the yoke of the Egyptians. And I bring (והבאתי) you to the land I swore with uplifted hand to give to Abraham, to Isaac and Jacob. I will give it to you as a possession. I am YHWH. (Ex. 6:7-8)

---

16. A. van Selms, *Marriage and Family Life in Ungaritic Literature* (London: Luzac & Co., 1954), 35, 37. *CTA* 14. 203-6.15. col. ii 21.

17. *tn nkl y* (18) *rḫ ytrḫ*.
   ib ʿarbm bbh (19) *th*.
   watn mhrh la (20) *bh*.

   Give Nikkal (that) Yarikh may marry (her)
   (give) Ib (that), she may enter into his mansion;
   And I will give as her bride-price to her father. . . (*CTA* 24.17-20)

This translation is from Gibson, *Canaanite Myths*, 128.
  18. Cf. NIV and NKJV.

YHWH, THE HUSBAND OF ISRAEL

These verses describe YHWH's election of Israel. The particular theological concept of election is expressed in marriage terms and formula, and YHWH's bringing of Israel to the promised land is portrayed by the imagery of a man bringing his bride into his home by using the Hebrew verb *bôʾ* (בוא).[19]

> "Return, faithless people," declares YHWH,
> for I am your husband (בעלתי)
> I will choose you (לקחתי)
> one from a town and two from a clan
> and bring you to Zion (והבואתי) . . . (Jer. 3:14)

"Faithless people" here refers to Israel. The relationship between YHWH and Israel is portrayed in terms of a father-son relationship. However, the relationship is changed to that of a husband and wife in the next line. It is clear that the concept of marriage is related to that of election since the marriage term *lāqaḥ* (לקח) is used as an election term and *bôʾ* (בוא) is used in the Hiphil form to denote the meaning of "bring." Thus, the image of YHWH's bringing Israel from Egypt to Canaan and Israel's following YHWH in the wilderness (Jer. 2:2-3) are similar to that of a bridegroom's bringing his bride to his house and bride's following her groom in marriage.[20]

4. *Hōšîḇ* (השיב, to marry, to settle)

The primary meaning of *Hōšîḇ* (השיב), the Hiphil form of *yāšaḇ* (ישב), is "to settle."

---

19. Sohn, 20-22.

20. It is to be noted here that the Hebrew verb *nāśaʾ* (נשא) itself does not clearly denote the relationship between YHWH and Israel. The usage of the word in Hos. 1:6 is vague.
> "Then she conceived again and she gave birth to a daughter.
> And YHWH said to him, 'Name he Loruhamah,
> For I will no longer have compassion on the house of Israel,
> That I indeed married to them (נשא אשא).'"

LXX reads *naśaʾ ʾeśaʾ* (נשא אשא) as ἀντιτασσόμενος ἀντιτάξομαι (surely array) and *BHS* proposes to read it as *naśaʾ ʾeśaʾ* (נשא אשא). However, "I indeed married to them" is most probable in view of context. See Michael DeRoche, "Jeremiah 2:2-3 and Israel's Love for God during the Wilderness Wandering," *CBQ* 45 (1983): 364-76.

The Marriage Terms

> So Joseph settled (וַיּוֹשֵׁב) his father and brothers and gave them possession in the land of Egypt, in the best of the land, in the land Rameses, as Pharaoh had ordered. (Gen. 47:11)

Joseph allotted his family a portion of the land of Egypt to take up a permanent residence. The Hiphil form of *yāšab* (יָשַׁב) is used for Israel's settlement in Egypt. However, in later Hebrew it is used to carry the meaning of "to marry."

> Do we hear about you that you have committed all this great evil by acting unfaithfully against our God by marrying (לְהֹשִׁיב) foreign women? (Neh. 13:27)

Since this usage is found only in Ezra and Nehemiah, it seems to have been used as a marriage term after the return from the exile. However, it is certainly an old custom in Israel to bring a woman and provide her a domicile. Isaac brought Rebekah from the land of Haran and led her "into his mother Sarah's tent, and he took her and she became his wife; and he loved her, thus Isaac was comforted after his mother's death" (Gen. 24:67). The shortage of housing due to an influx of population from Babylon and the culture of marriage which had been influenced by gentiles seem to be the main reasons for the use of this word as a marriage term after the exile.[21]

When *hōšîb* (הֹשִׁיב) is used to describe the relationship between YHWH and Israel, it refers to the idea of YHWH's settling Israel in the land of Canaan (1Sam. 12:8), or in cities (2 Kgs. 17:24, 26; Ezek. 36:33; 54:3; 2 Ch. 8:2), or in a house (Hos. 11:11; 12:10; Lev. 23:43).

5. *Hāyā lᵉ᾽ išā* (היה לאשה, *to be a wife*)

---

21. Cf. Neh. 13:23; Ezr. 10:2,10, 14,17, 18. According to H. G. M. Williamson, following T. Wilton Davis, this term is applied only to mixed marriage. Thus, the women whom the Israelites had living with them were harlots, not wives (*Ezra, Nehemiah* [Word Biblical Commentary; Waco, Texas: Word Books, 1985], 185). However, the contexts never say so, neither were their children and called "sons of harlotry" (ילדי זנונים) as in Hos. 1:2. If the women were harlots and their children sons of harlots, Nehemiah would not have rebuked them, beat them, and pulled out their hair because they could not understand Hebrew (Neh. 13:25).

YHWH, THE HUSBAND OF ISRAEL

The Hebrew verb *hāyā* (היה) does not carry the meaning of marriage. It simply means "to be," or "to become." However, the phrase *hāyā lᵉʾiššā* (היה לאשה) means "to be a wife of" or "to marry."

> Besides, she actually is my sister, the daughter of my father, but not the daughter of my mother, and she became my wife (ותהי־לי לאשה).(Gen. 20:12)

> Then the man who lay with her shall give to the girl's father fifty shekels of silver, and she shall become his wife (ולו־תהיה לאשה) because he has violated her, he cannot divorce her all his days. (Deut. 22:29)

Burrow says that the meaning of *hāyā lᵉʾ iššā* (היה לאשה) represents the loss of virginity and sometimes the physical relationship between man and woman.[22] *Hāyā* (היה) is often combined with marriage terms such as *lāqaḥ* (לקח) or *baʿal* (בעל). In this case, the man is the subject of *lāqaḥ* (לקח) and the woman is the subject of *baʿal* (בעל), constituting a part of the marriage formula.

> David also took Ahinoam of Jezreel, and they both became his wives (ואת־אחינעם לקח דוד מיזרעאל ותהיין גם־שתיהן לו לנשים). (1 Sam. 25:43; cf. Gen. 24:67; Deut. 24:4; 1 Sam. 25:40, 41; 2 Sam. 12:10; Ruth 4:13)

> She shall also remove the clothes of her captivity and shall remain in your house, and mourn her father and mother a full month; and after that you may go in to her and be her husband and she shall be your wife (ובעלתה והיתה לך לאשה). (Deut. 21:13)

Similar formulae such as "you are my wife" and "you are my husband,"[23] are found in the Old Testament. The Aramaic formula, "She is my wife and I her husband from this day forever" (הי אנתתי ואנה בעלה מן יומא זנה ועד עלם) is also a typical marriage contract which was found in Elephantine.[24] Yaron suggests that this kind of formula was used in Babylon in an advanced form

---

22. M. Burrow, 20.
23. M. A. Friedman, "Israel's Response in Hosea 2:17b: You Are My Husband," *JBL* 99/2 (1980): 199-204.
24. Cf. Brooklyn 2:4; 14:3-4. A. P. Cowley, *Aramaic Papyri of Fifth Century*, 44, 47-50.

in the later period.²⁵ An equivalent formula is also found in Tob. 7:11, where Sarah's father says to Tobias: "Henceforth thou art her brother and she is thy sister." Again, in a contract from the second century after Christ found in the Judean desert, the formula is "Thou shall be my wife."²⁶

Here it should also be noted that the usage of this formula is also applied to the YHWH-Israel relationship.

> Then I will take you for my people, and I will be your God (ולקחתי אתכם לי לעם והייתי לכם לאלהים); and you shall know that I am YHWH your God, who brought you out from under the burdens of the Egyptians. (Ex. 6:7)

In Hos. 2:23(Heb. 25) the marriage proclamation is directly applied to YHWH and Israel.

> I will say to those who were not my people,
> "You are my people!" (עמי־אתה)
> And they will say, "Thou art my God!" (אלהי)

Even though the verb *hayā* (היה) is not used, it is basically similar to the marriage formula, "She is my wife and I am her husband" (היא אשתי ואנכי אשה) and to the negative form of the divorce formula, "She is not my wife and I am not her husband" (ואנכי לא אשה היא לא אשתי). This formula will be dealt with later.

6. *ʾAraš* (ארש, to engage)

Generally, *ʾāraš* (ארש) is rendered as "to betroth" or "to engage."

> Who is the man that is engaged (ארש) to a woman and has not married her (לא לקח)? Let him depart and return to his house, lest he die in the battle and another man marry her. (Deut. 20:7; cf. 22:23, 25, 27, 28; 28:30; 2 Sam. 3:14)

---

25. R. Yaron, "Aramaic Marriage Contracts from Elephantine," *JSS* 31 (1958): 30-31.
26. R. De Vaux, *Ancient Israel* (2 vols.; New York: McGraw-Hill, 1961), 1:33.

It is evident here that the text differentiates between the meaning of *ʾāraš* (ארשׂ) and *lāqaḥ* (לקח). Whereas *ʾāraš* (ארשׂ) refers to engagement, *lāqaḥ* (לקח) refers to marriage. These have entirely different meanings. However, *ʾāraš* (ארשׂ) is used for marriage. Specifically, this term is used for the marriage relationship between YHWH and Israel in Hos. 2:19-20.

> And I will betroth you (ארשׂתיך) to me forever;
> Yes, I will betroth you (ארשׂתיך) to me in righteousness and in justice,
> In lovingkindness and in compassion,
> And I will betroth you (ארשׂתיך) to me in faithfulness.
> Then you will know YHWH.

Even though the NASB, NIV and other English versions translate *ʾāraš* (ארשׂ) as "to betroth" in these verses, the context points to the concept of marriage. Thus, Wolf regards it as a marriage term carrying the concept of possession and proposes the rendering of *ʾāraštik lî* (ארשׂתיך לי) as "I will make my own." According to Wolf, the Piel form of *ʾāraš* (ארשׂ) "marks the end of the premarital status, . . . in that it denotes the act of paying the bridal price (מהר), thus removing the last possible objection the bride's father might raise." Therefore, he distinguishes this term from *lāqaḥ* (לקח) or *šālaḥ* (שׁלח). Particularly, he points out that the text emphasizes the legal force of marriage by repeating the word three times here.[27] He properly understands this word as denoting a legal act constituting marriage.

7. Yāḏaʿ (ידע, *to know, to have sexual relation*)

Generally, *yāḏaʿ* (ידע) has been rendered as "to know." The objects of *yāḏaʿ* (ידע) cover almost all the areas of knowledge and information. Strictly speaking, this is not a marriage term. However, it is a relationship term. When used with regard to people, it denotes the concept of a personal and close relationship. When it is used between marriage partners, the term describes sexual relations, i.e., the most intimate human relationship.

---

27. H. W. Wolff, *Hosea* (Hermeneia; Philadelphia: Fortress, 1974), 52.

The Marriage Terms

> Now the man had relations with (ידע) his wife Eve, and she conceived and gave birth to Cain, and she said, "I have gotten a manchild with the help of YHWH." (Gen. 4:1)

The phrase here, "she conceived and gave birth to Cain" explains the nature of the relationship between Adam and Eve. Obviously, *yāda'* (ידע) describes the sexual relations between them.[28]

It is noteworthy that the relationship between YHWH and Israel is also described in terms of *yāda'* (ידע).

> For I have chosen (ידע) him, in order that he may command his children and his household after him to keep the way of YHWH by doing righteousness and justice; in order that YHWH may bring upon Abraham what he has spoken about him. (Gen. 18:19)

The NASB here renders *yāda'* (ידע) as "to choose." This rendering is more acceptable than the literal one "to know," or "to have a sexual relation." Speiser renders the term with the similar idea of "to single out."[29] This word is used to denote the idea of YHWH's election of Abraham.[30] It is a theological term. A similar example is found in the call narrative of Jeremiah. "Before I formed you in the womb I knew you (*yāda'tika*, ידעתיך)"(Jer. 1:5). The verb *yāda'* (ידע) is here obviously used as an election term, YHWH's choice of Jeremiah for the office of prophet before his birth. However, *yāda'* (ידע) is not limited to the individual as in the case of Abraham and Jeremiah. YHWH knew (ידע) Israel exclusively.

> You only have I known of all the families of the earth (לק אתכם ידעתי מכל משפחות האדמה): therefore I will punish you for all your iniquities. (Amos 3:2, KJV)

Consequently, YHWH asks Israel to know him only.

---

28. Besides *yāda'* (ידע), *rāba'* (רבע), *'innā* (ענה), and *šāgal* (שגל) are used as sexual terms in the Bible. However, *rāba'* (רבע) is used in the case of lying with beasts, the Piel form of *'innā* (ענה) in the case of rape, and *šāgal* (שגל) in the case of wife's lying with another man. The Masorets substituted this term with *šākab* (שכב) since it was regarded as distastful.

29. E. A. Speiser, *Genesis* (AB; Garden City: Doubleday,1964), 133.

30. Sohn, 24-26.

YHWH, THE HUSBAND OF ISRAEL

> Yet I have been YHWH your God
> Since the land of Egypt;
> And you were not to know (לא תדע) any god except me,
> For there is no savior besides me. (Hos. 13:4)

Therefore, Hosea exhorts his people "So let us know, let us press on to know YHWH"(ונדעה נרדפה לדעת את־יהוה, Hos 6:3). But *idû*, the Akkadian cognate of *yāḏaʿ* (ידע) does not carry the same meaning as its Hebrew counterpart.[31]

8. *Pāraś kanap* (פרש כנף, *to spread the skirt*)

When she was asked her identity lying at the feet of Boaz, Ruth replied, "I am Ruth your maid. So spread your covering (פרש כנף) over your maid, for you are a close relative."(Ruth 3:9). Since the Hebrew verb *pāraś kanap* (פרש כנף) means "to spread out (wings)," the literal translation of the verse is "to spread your wings over your maid." We are not sure of the exact meaning of this verse. However, it can be deduced from the context that it could have meant a kind of proposal of marriage or a request to bear a son to be the heir of her husband. Actually according to the Israelite custom and other ancient Near Eastern traditions, a man usually casts his clothes over the woman whom he wanted to marry.[32]

It is to be noted that this expression is also used in a theological context. In Ezek.16:8, YHWH says to Jerusalem, referring to Israel, "I spread my skirt over you and covered your nakedness" (ואפרש כנפי עליך ואכסה ערותך). Here *pāraś kanap* (פרש כנף) and *kāsaʿ erwā* (כסה ערוה) carry the same meaning as what Ruth said to Boaz. In relation to this expression, "to strip"(והפשיטו, Ezek. 23:36), "uncover nakedness" (גלה ערוה, Ezek. 16:36; 23:10), "remove the skirts and expose the heels" (וגם־אני חשפתי שוליך על־פניך ונראה קלונך, Jer.13:26), etc. are used to denote the idea of divorce. The Hiphil form of *pāšaṭ* (פשט) implies the concept of punishment since it is

---

31. Sohn, 26n. 36.
32. Mishnah Peah 4:3. Raphael Patai, *Sex and Family in the Bible and Middle East* (Garden City: Doubleday, 1959), 97.

usually used to strip off the skin of a man in the battle field. The Piel form of *galā* (גלה) simply means "to uncover," to bring to shame. Therefore, it is difficult to think that these terms were actually used in the process of divorce among the people of Israel and the ancient Near East. As the antithesis of "to cover" when depicting marriage, "to uncover" seems to be used to describe the idea of divorce.

9. Other Terms

In Ruth 4:10 *qānā* (קנה, to buy) is obviously a marriage term. *Nāṯan* (נתן) in Gen. 30:4; Judg. 21:7; 2 Kgs 14:9; 2 Ch. 25:18 is also used in the context of marriage. These words imply a marriage by purchase. However, in the case of Boaz, the meaning of the purchase was to acquire the right "to raise up the name of the deceased on his inheritance, so that the name of the deceased may not be cut off from his brothers and or from the court of his birth place." It was not a marriage by purchase in a strict sense. Sometimes, a girl was given (נתן) as a reward by her father to the one who accomplished a certain task such as in war. But this is hardly the case of the YHWH-Israel relationship.

The terms that we have observed express the typical aspects or characteristic elements of marriage. Thus we can deduce the meaning and custom of marriage from them. Marriage can be said to be a man's possession of woman. A husband became a master of wife through the ownership. Usually a husband went to the house of his would-be bride and he brought her to his house after paying the bridal price to her father. A marriage thus a kind of moving his dwelling place from her father's house to her husband's. As a result of the marriage the couple was permitted to know each other, that is to have sexual relation. And we have also observed that those marriage terms and concepts are similarly applied to YHWH-Israel relation. The people of Israel borrowed those marriage terms and ideas to describe their relationship with YHWH, their God.

CHAPTER II

The Marriage Formulae

Marriage was a kind of covenant between partners in Israel as well as in ancient Near Eastern society. Usually a wedding ceremony followed a meaningful ritual and a great festival, including a marriage proclamation which carried legal force.[1] The marriage proclamation was made by the married couple to announce their union as husband and wife. In the course of the wedding the proclamation occupied a very important place and followed a special format. Two kinds of marriage formula are observed. The declarative formula was used during the wedding by the groom or bride, and sometimes included a third person such as the father of the bride. The descriptive formula was used in a marriage contract or in describing the fact of marriage. These formulae adopted a special Hebrew syntax and are noteworthy since this formula was also used in the YHWH-Israel relationship.

1. THE DECLARATIVE FORMULAE

Three types of declarative formulae in marriage are observed in the ancient Near Eastern texts. First of all, it is reciprocal or mutual. The groom and bride declare to each other his or her relationship established through the marriage. "You are my wife," or "you are my husband" belongs in this category. This kind of formula can be observed from Old Babylonian legal documents.[2] The negative form of the marriage formula is used in the divorce formula, such as

---

1. S. Greengus, "The Babylonian Marriage Contract," *JAOS* 89. 3 (1969): 515.
2. G. P. Hugenberger, *Marriage as Covenant: A Study of Biblical Law & Ethic Covering Marriage, Developed from the Perspective of Malachi* (Leiden: E. J. Brill, 1994), 219n.13-17.

"you are not my wife" (*ul aššti atta*), "you are not my husband" (*ul muti atta*), "she (fPN) is not my wife," "he is not my husband," "I will not be your wife," and "you are not my wife, you are not my husband"(*ul ašštî attî, ul mutî atta*).³ These kinds of divorce formulae are observed more frequently than those of marriage in the ancient texts. It is natural to deduce here that the divorce formulae were derived from the marriage formula.

The second type is unilateral and one-sided. In this case, the groom or bride only declares the formula toward his or her counterpart. One of the well known declarative formulae of this type in the Old Babylonian period is from the Gilgamesh epic when *Ištar* proposes to Gilgamesh,

> "Come Gilgamesh, be thou my (var. an) espouser (var, groom); give me thy charms for a gift; be thou my husband, I will be thy wife." (*attā lū mutîa anau lū aššîka*) (vi 7-9) ⁴

A cuneiform text from Nippur of ancient Babylonia records the marriage contract as follows:

> If Awiliya says to Naramtum his wife, "You are not my wife," he will pay 1/2 mina of silver. If Naramtum says to Awiliya her husband, "You are not my husband," he will shave her and place a slave mark on her and give her for silver.⁵

---

3. G. F. Hugenberger, 219. n. 13-17. *BAP* 89: 20-23, 36-38; 90:11-12; *BIN* 7 173:16-29; Böhl Leiden Collection 772:6-10; *CT* 2 44:6-16; 8 7b :13-16; Kich 1 B17:10'-17' ; *PBS* 8/2 252:18-26; *TIM* 4 46:5'-17', 47:16-25, 48:8ff, 49: rev 1'-4'(beginning broken); *YOS* 12 371:6-15. Cf. Greengus, 517n. 58.

4. A similar passage appears in the myth of Nergal and Ereshkigal; the queen of the netherworld, threatened by Nergal, pleads for her and says:

"You be my husband, I will be thy wife . . .
Be thou master, I will be mistress."

(*attā lu muti$_{ma}$ ^{I}anāku lū aššîka . . .
attā lū bēlu anāku lū bēltu*) (EA 375:82-85)

5. *tukun-bi ^{I}a-wi-li-ya na-ra-am-tum dam-a-ni-ra dam-mu nu-me-en ba-na-an-du $_{II}$ 1/2 ma-na kù-babbar i-lá-e*

tukun-bi ^{I} na-am-tum a-wi-li-ya dam-a-ni-ra dam-mu nu-me-en ba-na-an-du $_{II}$ umbin al-ku5 ru-dè kù-šebi-ib-sum-mu-uš

Babylonian Expedition of the University of Pennsylvania, Series A: Cuneiform Texts (Philadelphia: Department of Archaeology, University of Pennsylvania). 6/2 Arno Poebel, *Babylonian*

The Marriage Formula

"You are not my wife,"or "You are not my husband" is obviously the negative form of the marriage formula. These kinds of divorce formulae presuppose the existence of a marriage formula. This one-sided declarative formula in marriage is also found in the well-known Elephantine papyrus. In the papyrus, the groom usually proclaims: "She is my wife and I am her husband from this day and forever"(הי אנתתי ואנה בעלה מן יומא זנה עד עלם).[6]

The third type of formula is an indirect one. The third person pronounces the declarative formula. *TIM* 4 45:1-9 from the Middle Assyrian document is a good example.

> "PN and ͨPN of their own accord agreed to marriage; PN is her husband ͨPN is his wife. They shall show respect to one another at home and abroad."[7]

This text shows that a third person other than the couple pronounces the declarative formula in marriage. It is not certain who declared the formula in

---

Legal and Business Documents from the Time of the First Dynasty of Babylon, Chiefly from Nippur (1902). 6/2 48. cited in Elezabeth C. Stone and David L. Owen, *Adoption in Old Babylon Nippur and the Archive of Mannum-mes-liṣṣur* (Winona Lake: Eisenbrauns, 1991), 51-52. Following is found among the Late Sumerian Marriage Contract:

> "If Enlil-izzu ever says to Ama-sukkal, his wife, 'You are no longer my wife,' he shall return the 19 shekels of silver and he shall also weigh out 1/2 mina as her divorce settlement. On the other hand, if Ama-sukkal ever says to Enil-izzu, her husband, 'You are no longer my husband,' she shall forfeit the 19 shekels of silver and she shall also weigh out 1/2 mina of silver. In mutual agreement they have sworn together by king." (The names of eight men, two women, the scribe, and the notary as witness, each preceded by the witness sign.) (Sealed with two seals, twice each).

Published and translated by A. Poebel, *Babylonian Business and Legal Documents* (1909), No. 40. cited in *ANET*, 219.

6. Bezalel Porten and Ada Yardeni, *Textbook of Aramaic Documents From Ancient Egypt*, Volume 2: Contract, The Hebrew University Department of the History of the Jewish People. *Texts and Studies for Students* (Jerusalem : Hebrew University, 1989), B2. 6, 4. Cf. B3.3; 3f. B3.8, 4; B6.1, 3f. Cf. Cowley, *Aramaic Papyri 15:3f*; Kraeling, *Brooklyn Museum Aramaic Papyri 2:3f*, 7:4; 14:4f. R. De Vaux, *Ancient Israel* (New York: McGraw-Hill, 1966), vol. 1., 33

7. PN ū ͨPN ina migratišnu mutūtu ū ašštūta idbubū PN mussa

ū ͨPN aššassu ina eqli ū libbi ā[lim] palāḫa aḫu a[ḫa] ippuššū

Greengus, 521n. 75. Cf. Hugenberger, 223.

this case, but it was possibly either the father of the bride or the head of the tribe.

In the Ancient Near East, a marriage was a kind of contract which carried legal force, and a marriage document was to be drawn up by both partners. The code of Eshnunna required a formal marriage contract if a man and woman were to obtain full social and legal recognition of their marriage.[8] The code of Hammurabi acknowledges only those marriages for which contracts had been drawn up.[9] In Egypt it was common practice to write a marriage contract.[10] This concept of marriage as a covenant is also found among the Israelites in Gen. 31:50 and Mal 2:14.[11] Tobit 7:12 shows that the covenant documents in marriage were drawn up even after the Biblical period.[12] In Mishnah, the marriage document was known as *ketubba*.

According to Greengus, however, the marriage contract which was required in the Code of Eshnunna and the Code of Hammurabi is not necessarily a written document. He asserts that the term *riksātum* can be translated as a "binding agreement, pact, covenant," or in a broad sense "contract," but *prima facie* there is nothing in the terms *riksātum* or *rakāsum* to indicate a written document.[13] If this is correct, the declarative formula itself can be said to have carried the legal force as the written document did.

---

8. §27 If a man took another man's daughter without asking her father and mother and did not arrange for a libation and marriage contract with her father and mother and though she live in his house for a year, she is not a wife. § 28 If . . . he arranged for a marriage contract and libation with her father and mother and took her, she is his wife; the day she is caught with (another) man she shall die; she shall not live. Quoted from "The Old Babylonian Marriage Contract" *JAOS* 89.3 (1969): 505.

9. "If a seignor acquired a wife, but did not draw up the contract for her, that woman is no wife." The Code of Hammurabi § 128. *Ancient Near Eastern Texts Relating to the Old Testament,* ed. James B. Pritchard (Princeton: Princeton University Press, 1969), 171.

10. Nathaniel Reich, "Marriage and Divorce in Ancient Egypt: Papyrus Documents Discovered at Thebes by the Eckly B. Coxe Jr. Expedition to Egypt," *The Museum Journal* (Philadelphia: University of Pennsylvania, 1924): 50-57.

11. A thorough research of Gordon Paul Hugenberger on Mal 2:14 shows that in the Bible marriage was regarded as covenant. *Marriage as Covenant: A Study of Biblical Law & Ethic Covering Marriage, Developed from the perspective of Malachi* (Leiden: E.J. Brill, 1994).

12. On marriage in Tobit, see P. Grelot, "The Institution of Marriage: Its Evolution in the Old Testament," *Concillium* 55 (1970): 39-50

13. Greengus, 506.

The Marriage Formula

The declarative formula in marriage also can be regarded as the covenant. The oral declaration effected the bond and defined the nature of the relationship. In order to carry legal force, this declaration was always made in the presence of an official assembly as its witness.[14] A Middle Assyrian Law, KAV I.vi: 1-5 (*ANET*, 183) regulated the number of witnesses required stating that five or six neighbors should be brought as witnesses in order to veil the concubine, and that he must say "she is my wife" in their presence. This means that the marriage declaration was to be made before the public in order to ratify the marriage union. One observation to be noted here is that all these declarative formulae are constituted in a nominal clause, i.e. a verbless sentence.

Now we can return to the Bible and see how these declarative formulae are related to Biblical marriage formulae and covenant formulae. In Hos. 2:4 (E. 2:2), YHWH asks the children of Gomer to contend with their mother and said, "for she is not my wife, and I am not her husband"(כי־היא לא אשתי ואנכי לא אישה). This is apparently modeled upon a marriage formula similar to the one used in the Elephantine: "She is my wife and I am her husband from this day and forever" (הי אנתתי ואנהבעלה מן יומא זנה עד עלם). Along with this understanding, the rejection formula in Hos. 1:9 draws our attention. "And YHWH said, 'Name him Loammi, for you are not my people and I am not your God'"(קרא שמו לא עמי כי אתם לא עמי ואנכי לא־אהיה לכם). This is exactly the same divorce formula that was used in Old Babylon, "You are not my wife, I am not you husband" (*ul aššti atti, ul muti attā*). The rejection formula in Hos. 2:1 (E. 1:10): "You are not my people"(לא עמי אתה) is also a modification of the declarative formula of divorce:"You are not my husband"(*ul muti atta*) used in the ancient Near East. YHWH's rejection of his people is described in terms of a husband's denouncement of his wife. The conformity of the rejection formula in the Bible to the divorce formula in the ancient Near East brings to light the conformity of the marriage formula with the covenant formula. In view of this, "You are my people" and "Thou art my God" in Hos. 2:23 is modified from the reciprocal proclamation formula in marriage. YHWH's proposal of marriage to Israel in Hos. 2:19-20 clearly supports this understanding. The covenant formula, "I will be your God and you will be my people" is also modified from the proclamation

---

14. Kalluveetil, 110.9.

formula of marriage, "You will be my wife and I will be thy husband."

One point to be noted in this parallelism is that the covenant formula is not a nominal clause as the declarative formula in marriage. The verb *hāyā* (היה) plays a key role in the covenant formula. *Hāyā* (היה) simply means "to be," or "to become." According to Ogden's research, *hāyā* (היה) is mainly used (1) to connect words as a coupula, (2) to indicate the existence of a subject, and (3) to indicate the transition from one sphere of existence to another.[15] According to his classification, the use of *hāyā* (היה) in this case is both connecting and transitional in describing the concept of covenant. As a connecting word it establishes a relationship and by taking the preposition *lamed* (ל) twice, it specifies the direction of the transition (לו) and the relationship between the subject and the predicate (לאשא). Therefore, we do not find any syntactical difference between the marriage formula and the covenant formula. This means that "You are my people" and "Thou art my God" are basically covenant ratifying formulae, such as "I will be your God and You will be my people," and these covenant formulae between YHWH and Israel originated from the marriage formulae (15a). In particular, Deut. 26:17-19 ("You have declared YHWH, this day to be your God . . . and YHWH has declared you, this day, to be his treasured people") seems to be the most convincing evidence that the covenant formula is a reflection of a mutual declaration in marriage.[16]

2. THE DESCRIPTIVE FORMULAE

Along with the declarative formula in marriage, the descriptive formula in marriage was used in the ancient Near East. The descriptive formula of marriage is distinguished from the declarative formula by its usage and form. The descriptive formula of marriage is usually used for a written document.

---

15. G. S. Ogden, "Time and the Verb היה in O.T. Prose," *VT* 21 (1971): 451

16. Mordecai A. Friedman, "Israel's Response in Hoea 2:17b: 'You are my husband,'" *JBL* 99/2 (1980): 199-204.

The Marriage Formula

Unlike the declarative formula, the groom or a third person describes or explains that the marriage relationship was established between the partners and that they have entered into a bond that is legally binding.

Among the descriptive formulas of marriage in the Hebrew Bible, "X (man) took Y(woman) for his wife" (לקח X(מ) את־Y ל־X לאשה) and "X took Y and Y became his wife" (לקח X [מ] את־Y ותהי־ל־X לאשה) are the most frequently used.[17] One of the best examples for the first formula is found in Ex. 6:20.

ויקח עמרם את־יוכבד דודתו לו לאשה:
Amram married his father's sister Jochebed. (NIV)[18]

Here we can see the verb *lāqaḥ* (לקח) takes the inseparable preposition *lamed* (ל) twice. The first denotes the direction of transference, while the second one indicates the reason for the taking. Thus, Amram takes Jochebed unto him for the purpose of her becoming his wife. However, two sentences are joined in the second formula and the inseparable preposition *lamed* (ל) led twice by the verb *hāyā* (היה).[19]

ויקח בעז את־רות ותהי־לו לאשה
Boaz took Ruth and she became his wife (Ruth 4:13)[20]

As a modification of this formula, *watehî* (ותהי) is replaced with *liheyot* (להיות), the infinitive form of *hāyā* (היה). Then the formula is לקח X(מ) את־Y להיות ל־X לאשה (X took Y to be his wife).

ועתה לא־תסור חרב מביתך עד־עולם עקב כי בזתני
ותקח את־אשת אוריה החתי להיות לך לאשה:
Now therefore, the sword shall never depart from your house, because you

---

17. Sohn, *The Divine Election of Israel*, 31-32.
18. Cf. Gen.25:20; 34:4, 21; Ex. 6:20, 23, 25; Dt. 21:11; 25:5; Judg. 3:6; 1 Sam. 25:39, 40; 2 Sam. 5:9; Ezek. 44:22.
19. See Good's *The Sheep of His Pasture*, pp. 65-68 for an extensive discussion about the life setting of this formula . . . היה ל־. . . ל־.
20. Cf. Gen. 24:67; 1 Sam. 25:43.

have despised me and have taken the wife of Uriah the Hittite to be your wife. (2 Sam. 12:10) [21]

It is important to an understanding of marriage in the Bible to realize that the descriptive formulae of marriage are formulated by the Hebrew verb *lāqaḥ* (לקח) and taking the inseparable preposition *lamed* (ל) twice. *Lāqaḥ* (לקח) is a marriage term like בעל, נשא, הושיב, בוא, קנה, and ארש, etc.[22] The Semitic root form *lāqaḥ* (לקח) is extensively used as a marriage term in the ancient Near East. *Leqû*, the Akkadian cognate of *lāqaḥ* (לקח), is also a marriage term with *aḫāzum*. *Lqḥ*, the Ugaritic cognate also carries the same meaning. However, these cognates do not have the syntactical similarity with the Hebrew verb *lāqaḥ* (לקח) by taking *lamed* (ל) twice.[23] The Hebrew descriptive formula of marriage is a unique one. Basically, *lāqaḥ* (לקח) carries the concept of possession by either agreement or capture. The subject (X) of the verb possesses (לקח) the object Y for the purpose of X's wife (אשה). A wife was the special property of her husband.[24] Marriage was a kind of declarative ceremony of the groom's ownership of his bride.

Surprisingly enough, this descriptive formula of marriage is used for the relationship between YHWH and his people. The people of Israel employed the imagery of marriage to describe their intimate relationship with YHWH. They used the marriage term *lāqaḥ* (לקח) as an election term and modified the marriage formula for the election formula.[25] As an election formula, "I will take you for my people and I will be your God," or "YHWH has taken you to be a people for his own possession" is frequently found in the Hebrew Bible.

ולקחתי אתכם לי לם והייתי לכם לאלהים וידעתם כי
אני יהוה אלהיכם המוציא אתכם מתחת סבלות מצרים.

---

21. See also Deut. 24:4.
22. Sohn, 10-29.
23. The Akkadian literature describes it in simple sentence, *RN mārat RN$_2$ and DAM-ut-ti-šu il-te-qè* (*Ammistamru* took the daughter of *Benteśma* as his wife). MRS 9 126 RS 17, 159:6. quoted fr. *CAD*, L. 137.
24. Sohn, 18-19.
25. Sohn, 33-37.

The Marriage Formula

Then I will take you for my people, and I will be your God and you shall know that I am YHWH your God, who brought you out from under the burdens of the Egyptians. (Ex. 6:7)

The wording of the election formula, "ולקחתי אתכם לי לעם והייתי לכם לאלהים" (I will take you for my people and I will be your God) is in accordance with the marriage formula (לקח [x]ן X את־Y ותהי־לי־X לאשה) except for the substitution of the pronoun, ʾam (עם, people) and ʾelohi m (אלהים, God). The modified formula (לקח[x]ן את־Y להיות לי X לאשה) is found in Duet. 4:20.

ואתכם לקח יהוה ויוצא אתכם מכור הברזל ממצרים
להיות לו לעם נחלה כיום הזה:

But YHWH has taken you and brought out of the iron furnace, from Egypt, to be a people for his own possession, as today. (Deut. 4:20)

The formula, ואתכם לקח יהוה ... להיות לו לעם נחלה (YHWH has taken you ... to be a people for his own possession) is also in accordance with the descriptive formula of marriage: "YHWH has taken you to be his people," or "I will take you for my people and I will be your God." As the marriage was a declaration of the groom's ownership of his bride, YHWH also proclaims ownership of Israel as his special possession. Israel is described as ʿam segulā (עם סגלה, Deut. 7:6; 14:2; 26:18; cf., Ex. 19:5; Mal. 3:17; Ps. 13:4) and ʿam naḥalā (עם נחלה, Deut. 4:20; 1 Kgs 8:35). The word naḥalā (נחלה) is derived from the verb nāḥal (נחל) which means "to possess." Most English versions render the term as "inheritance." However, the Ugaritic cognate nḥlt also has the concept of possession. The realm of Mot is called arṣ nḥlt (the land of his possession)[26] and Sapan, the holy mountain of Baal's sanctuary, as ǵnḥlt (the mountain of my possession).[27] In view of the above, the rendering of ʿam naḥalā (עם נחלה) as "the people of possession" is more desirable than "the people of inheritance." Segulā (סגלה), carrying the meaning of "valued property," is essentially the same as naḥalā (נחלה). According to Rogers, the term segulā (סגלה) is always used to refer to the elected group in Biblical Hebrew, whereas naḥalā (נחלה) is not.[28] The Akkadian cognate sug kullu

---

26. *CTA* 4. VIII 13-14.
27. *CTA* 3. III 27.

carries the meaning of "herd." [29] In the ancient Near Eastern nomadic societies the herd or flock would be counted as valued property. Therefore, *ʿam naḥalā* (עם נחלה) and *ʿam segulā* (עם סגלה) carry the concept of possession. As *loʾišā* (לאשה) carries the concept of property or possession in the marriage formula of לקח את־Y ל־X לאשה, in the election formula it also carries the same concept of possession. The election formula seems to add *naḥalā* (נחלה) and *segulā* (סגלה) to *ʿam* (עם) in order to clarify the concept of possession.

Based on this analogy, the concept and formulae of a covenant expressing an intimate relationship between Yahweh and Israel are essentially same as those in marriage. However, many of the commentators regard Ex. 6:7 as the covenant formula, since the latter part of the formula (I will be your God) echoes the covenant formula (You will be my people and I will be your God).[30] The election formula is not always in conformity with the covenant formula. YHWH elected Israel from the land of Egypt and made the covenant with them at Mount Sinai; thus, he became the God of Israel and Israel became the people of YHWH. YHWH and Israel entered into this mutual relationship through election, and they entered into a legal bond through the covenant. As a result, the covenant carries legal force along with mutual responsibilities and obligations. The election necessarily entails the covenant in order to carry the legal force. The election and covenant always go together. Without election, there is no covenant, and if there is election, the covenant naturally follows. Therefore, the election formula and the covenant formula are used interchangeably throughout the Bible. This makes it difficult to make a clear distinction between election and covenant in their formulae. However, the significant point here is that the YHWH-Israel relationship,

---

28. R. G. Rogers, "The Doctrine of Election in the Chronicler's Work and Dead Sea Scrolls" (Ph. D. Dissertation, Boston University, 1969), 108.

29. *AHw* 2:1053f. *CAD.* vol. 15, 345. See also E. Klein, *A Comprehensive Etymological Dictionary of the Hebrew Language for the Readers of English* (New York: Macmillan, 1987), 434.

30. J. L. Durham regards this as a "covenant promise." *Exodus* (WBC 3; Waco: Word Books, 1987), 78. J. P. Hyatt believes that "the fundamental idea of covenant relationship is expressed here." *Commentary on Exodus* (NCC; London: Oliphants, 1971), 94. Cf. Alan Cole, *Exodus* (TOTC; London: Tyndale Press, 1973), 86. M. Noth calls it a "covenant formula." *Exodus: A Commentary* (OTL; London: SCM Press, 1962), 60.

whether it is election or covenant, is described in marriage terms and marriage formulae.

From the above observation, the relationship between the marriage formula and the covenant formula is clear. Many scholars, however, have traced the origin of the concept of a biblical covenant back to the international political treaties of the ancient Near East. The points of agreement between the content and form of the Hittite treaty and those of a biblical covenant provide a good basis for this assertion. However, it seemed easier for the people of Israel to describe their relationship with YHWH in terms of a marriage rather than using the form and content of an international political treaty in the ancient Neat East. Obviously, the marriage concept contains a more abundant, realistic and deeper meaning for describing the relationship.

Moreover, Good proposes that the origin of the covenant formula is fashioned after a client formula, the adoption of a tribe by an individual as seen especially in Arabic culture. According to Good, in ancient times among the Arabs the rule for a client relationship was expressed by the phrase *aṭ-ṭunub biṭ-ṭunub* (tent rope touching tent rope).[31] The joining of tents established a client relationship. Thus, the formula became "We encompassed their tents with our tents, and they became our 'cousin'(*banu ʿamm*)." Thus he concludes: "That a client formula should circulate with a tent is entirely appropriate. The joining of YHWH's tents to Israel accomplishes exactly what the covenant formula expresses: the adoption of a tribe by its new deity. The association of formula and tabernacle thus appears to primary."[32]

It is true that Good does not ignore the similarity between the nomad's custom of adoption into a tribe by the attaching of a tent rope and the Israelite practice of pitching their tents around YHWH's tabernacle. But Israel's pitching of their tents around YHWH's tabernacle should be understood from a different perspective. YHWH says in Ex. 29:45-46, "Then I will dwell among the Israelites and be their God. They will know that I am YHWH their God, who brought them out of Egypt so that I might dwell among them. I am YHWH their God." Since YHWH's deliverance of Israel and making the covenant on Mount Sinai are explained in terms of the marriage metaphor as

31. R. M. Good, *The Sheep of His Pasture*, 83.
32. Ibid., 84

given above, YHWH's dwelling among the Israelites can be compared to that of a newly wedded couple in their new home. YHWH's dwelling in the midst of Israel reinforces the analogy of a marriage relationship between them. The visible symbol of his residence among the Israelites was his tabernacle placed in the midst of Israel's tents and the people of Israel understood the presence of YHWH through the tabernacle's existence among them. The YHWH-Israelite relationship is far more intimate and binding in its nature than the tribal relationship of the client formula as Good proposed.

Summing up the above discussion, the terms and formula of the covenant are in accordance with that of a marriage. Even the ideas implied in marriage and a covenant are parallel to each other. This leads us to conclude that the origin and background of the covenant is the marriage practice among the people of Israel. The people of Israel employed marriage terms and imagery to describe their intimate and dynamic relationship with YHWH. Along with this analogy, it can be concluded that the rejection formula, "You are not my people, and I am not your God," is derived from the divorce formula, "She is not my wife, and I am not her husband." In addition, the origin of the restoration formula, "I will be your God and you will be my people," can be traced back to the election formula and further to the marriage formula. Therefore, the relationship between YHWH and Israel is described in terms of marriage, its formulae, and the customs of the ancient Near East, particularly those of Palestine. Falk correctly pointed out that covenant formula was associated with Israel's marital-covenantal response formula ("You are my wife," "You are my husband.") which was to be declared by both partners.[33] In particular, Friedman's assertion is very persuasive that the covenant form of Deut. 26:17-19 ("You have declared YHWH, this day, to be your God ... and YHWH has declared you, this day, to be his treasured people.") is a reflection of mutual declaration in marriage.[34]

---

33. Z. W. Falk, *Hebrew Law in Biblical Times* (Jerusalem: Wahrmann, 1964), 135.
34. M. A. Friedman, "Israel's Response in Hosea 2:17b: 'You are my husband,'" *JBL* 99/2 (1980): 199-204. Sohn, *The Divine Election of Israel*, 188-89. R. Smend, *Die Bundesformel* (1963); idem, *Die Mitte des Alten Testaments* (1970) 49-54; N. Lohfink, "Deut. 26:17-19 und die Bundesformel," *Zeitschrift für katholische Theologie* 91 (1969): 517-53, Hugenberger, 180n.58. M. Weinfeld, "ברית," *TDOT*, 2:278.

CHAPTER III

The Marriage in Israel

In the previous chapter we have noted that the marriage terms and formulae used among the Israelites are employed to denote the relationship between YHWH and themselves. The people of Israel understood and explained their close relationship with YHWH in terms of the relationship of a married couple. Therefore, our next step is to examine the marriage customs and regulations in ancient Israel including the engagement, married life, divorce and even remarriage in order to better understand their intimate relationship with YHWH.

1. THE ENGAGEMENT IN ISRAEL

Two customs seem to have existed as ways for a man to take his wife in ancient Semitic society. One way was that the parents of both partners selected or decided who would be the spouse of their children. In this case, the bridegroom usually paid the bridal price to the father of the bride and brought her as a wife to his home. The other way was that a man on the battlefield captured a girl in war and took her as his wife.

These two customs were also practiced in Israel. Abraham sent his old servant to his hometown to take a wife for his son, Isaac. Jacob served Laban, his uncle, for fourteen years to earn Leah and Rachel for his wives (Gen. 29:18). Caleb gave his daughter Acsah to Othniel in marriage in fulfillment of his promise to give her to the man who attacked and captured Kiriath Sepher (Josh. 15:16-17). David also brought one hundred foreskins of the Philistines to Saul in order to marry his daughter Michal (1 Sam. 18:27). The Scripture regulates a marriage by capture on the battlefield. The Bible commands the soldiers of Israel to kill all the men in the city they captured. However, it was permitted to save the lives of women and children and take them as slaves. Particularly, if they wished to take wives from among the captured women, they could do so according to the regulations in the Law. In that case the process of manumission was required (Deut. 21:11-12). Scholars' opinions are divergent on the issue as to whether this kind of custom actually existed in the history of Israel. However, we can find some indication of this occurrence in Judg. 21. Even though the event of the Benjamites taking wives from the daughters of Shiloh during the feast time is an unusual case in the Bible, the dialogue between the tribal leaders illustrate that they had a custom of marriage by capture.

> When their fathers or brothers complain to us, we will say to them, "Do us a kindness by helping them, because we did not get wives for them during the war, and you are innocent, since you did not give your daughters to them." (Judg. 21:22)

The phrase, "because we did not get wives for them during the war," implies the custom of marriage by capture. However, marriage by capture cannot be said to be the norm because war did not regularly occur, and they could not periodically wage war in order to take women for wives. Therefore, it is our understanding that marriage arranged by the parents was the ordinary means of taking wives in Israel.

After the process of selecting a spouse, the next step was engagement. In Israel there seemed to be a custom of engagement, since the Hebrew words denoting the idea *ʾaraś* (ארש, to engage or to betroth) and *kelûot* (כלולת, engagement, or the state of engagement) are found. The engagement of the Patriarchs varies from person to person. There is no mention of Abraham's engagement to Sarah. For Isaac, the period of engagement did not last long since Rebekah followed the old servant of Abraham immediately after her match was established. However, for Jacob it took seven years for him to take his wife after their engagement.

The engagement usually carried the same legal force as marriage. A man who was engaged was free from military service (Deut. 20:7) and an engaged girl who slept with another man was stoned to death as in the case of a married woman (Deut. 22:23-27). De Vaux suggested that at the time of engagement the bridal price was decided. After the father of the bride received the amount of money, he might possibly proclaim, "Today you shall be my son-in-law" (1Sam. 18:21).[1] The purpose of this period between engagement and marriage was to give an opportunity for each partner to withdraw from it in the event that any objections were raised. Of course, in that case, proper compensation had to be made from the party who withdrew from the engagement. In the New Testament Joseph and Mary had the status of being engaged and were not yet permitted to sleep together. Thus, Joseph was irritated when he found her pregnant (Matt.1:19).

2. THE MARRIAGE IN ISRAEL

Once each partner decided on his or her would-be-spouse, the next step was the wedding ceremony. It was one of the greatest feasts within the community to which they belonged. A marriage feast seems to imply many important points. First of all, the marriage partners were acknowledged as a married couple within their family and community through the wedding feast. Their friends and relatives would congratulate them and bless their marriage on this occasion. The legal binding of the male and female as a husband and wife was effective from this point of the wedding. Therefore, one of the most important elements in a wedding was the marriage proclamation by the bridegroom toward his bride and the people invited. The bride was a possession of her father up to this point. That was the reason for her to be obedient to her father, particularly to accept the groom that her father has chosen. However, through the wedding the right of possession of the bride is transferred from her father to her husband. The bridegroom proclaimed this publicly, "You are my wife and I am your husband from now on until forever." This marriage declaration obviously reflects the idea of possession and transference. The bridegroom proclaims not only the fact of the marriage status but also the legal right of possession of the woman as his bride through the declaration. The Hebrew word for husband *baʾal* (בעל) whose meaning is

---

1. R. de Vaux, *Ancient Israel: Its Life and Institutions* (London: Darton, Longman & Todd, 1961), 32-33.

"possessor" or "master" also reflects this concept (Hos. 2:18; Gen. 20:3; Ex. 21:2, 22; Lev. 21:4; Deut. 22:24; 2 Sam. 11:26; Joel 1:18). The custom that a wife is called by the name of her husband also seems to carry the same idea (Isa. 4:1).

In the wedding ceremony, the marriage proclamation was followed by the marriage covenant. The marriage covenant seems to have contained a typical form and content, such as the names of the married couple, the bridal price, the regulations regarding divorce, etc.[2] The significance of drawing up the covenant document was to enforce the legal nature of the marriage. Thus, the wedding guests were obviously witnesses to the marriage.

After the ceremony the new couple went into their chamber. In Hebrew this idea is expressed by the phrase $bô^\jmath$ $^\jmath lêha$ (בוא אליה), whose meaning is the groom's "going in to his bride." After seven years of service Jacob went to Laban, his uncle, and said, "Give me my wife, for my time is completed, that I may go in to her" (אבואה אליה, Gen. 29:21). Samson also went to his father-in-law and told him, "I will go in to my wife in her room" (אבואה אל־אשתי החדרה, Judg. 15:1). Both phrases, "to go in to her," or "to go in to my wife," describe the sexual union of the married couple. Speiser correctly pointed out that the Hebrew word $bō^\jmath$ (בוא) must be translated "to unite with," or "to cohabit with," since it describes the groom's going in to the room where his bride is waiting for him on the night of their wedding.[3] A similar word for this usage, $yada^c$ (ידע) is found. The lexical meaning of this word is "to know." However, in many cases this term is used to denote the sexual union between the married couple. The Hebrew word $sākaḇ$ (שכב, to lie) also carries the same meaning as $yāḏa^c$ (ידע), but it is usually used for the illegal case or for the couple outside of marriage (Gen. 19:32, 34, 35; 26:10; 34:2,7; 35:22; 39:7, 12, 14; Ex. 22:15; Deut. 22:22; 2 Sam. 11:4, 11; 12:11, 24; 13:11, 14). As is seen in Gen. 4:1, "Now the man had relations (ידע) with his wife Eve and she conceived (הרה) and gave birth to (ילד) Cain

---

2. The Code of Hammurabi, #128. The Code of Eshnuna, #27, 28. de Vaux, 33.
3. E. A. Speiser, *Genesis* (Anchor Bible; Garden City: Doubleday, 1964), pp. 44, 225. Cf. Gen. 6:4; 16:2; 29:23; 30:3; 38:8,9; 39:14; Deut. 22:13; Judg. 16:1; 2 Sam. 12:24; 16:21; 20:3; Ezek. 23:44; Prov. 6:29. etc.

and she said, 'I have gotten a man child with the help of YHWH,'" *yāḏaʿ* (ידע) is usually followed by the verb, *harā* (הרה) and *yālaḏ* (ילד) and this clarifies its meaning. Since the young Israelites married with whom their parents appointed or selected, the term "to love" (אהב) is usually used for married couples (Gen. 24:67; 29:18, 32; Judg. 14:16; 16:15; 1 Sam. 1:15; 1 Kgs 11:1; Esth. 2:17). The bride should be a virgin and she was to prove her virginity on the first night. The evidence of her virginity was to be kept for the possible case of accusation raised by her husband at a later time (Deut. 22:13-21). The marriage feast was usually held in the house of the bridegroom for seven days (Matt. 22:2; Gen. 29:27; Judg.14:12). The guests blessed the new couple and praised their good character and virtue (Jer. 16:9). Psalm 45 and the Song of Songs seem to have been written based on the background of the marriage feast.

3. THE MARRIAGE LIFE IN ISRAEL

After the wedding feast the couple officially became husband and wife, and they were legally bound to each other, sharing the responsibilities and obligations as members of a new family. The husband was to prepare a tent or house for his wife. Isaac took Rebekah as his wife and brought her into his mother's tent (Gen. 24:67). In addition, the husband was to provide his wife with food and clothes (Hos. 2:5; Isa. 4:1). Furthermore, a husband was to be her patron and was responsible for her status and legal standing in every area of her life (Num. 30:10). Thus Ruth 1:9 and 3:1 describe the marraige as finding "a resting place"(מנוח) for a woman.

However, the wife's obligations to her husband were much heavier than those of her husband. First of all, a wife was responsible for bearing children for her husband. This was especially true in regard to bearing a son. In the case of barrenness, a wife was to take a concubine for her husband and have her bear a child, as in the case of Sarah for Abraham, so that the family line would not be cut off (Gen. 16).[4] When a husband died at an early age and left

---

4. According to E. A. Speiser, this custom is found in a text from Nuzi. "If Gilimninu bears children, Shennima shall not take another wife. But if Gilimninu fails to bear children, Gilimninu shall get for Dhennima a woman from the Lullu country (i.e., a slave girl) as a con-

no children, the widow was to have relations with one of her husband's brothers and bear a son and raise up the name of her deceased husband on earth (Gen. 38; Ruth 4:5). The formula of a birth announcement, such as "X (the name of wife) bore Z (the name of son) to Y (the name of husband)" (X ילדה בן Z ל Y), also reflects the idea of the wife's obligation to bear a child for her husband. [5]

The second obligation required for a wife to fulfill was "faithfulness." She was not allowed to know(ידע) any other man but her husband. The Seventh Commandment prohibits adultery (Ex. 20:14; Deut. 5:18). In Lev. 20:10, the capital punishment was imposed upon a couple who committed adultery. A betrothed woman was regarded as a married woman in regard to the issue of adultery. The Bible commands that a couple involved in the crime of adultery be stoned (Deut. 22:23 f.). When Judah was informed that his daughter-in-law, Tamar, bore a child as a result of her harlotry, he commanded that she be brought out and burned (Gen. 38:24). Perfect loyalty to her husband was required, and this was considered as the obligation and virtue of a wife.

4. THE DIVORCE IN ISREAL

As has been observed in marriage, a husband takes the initiative and leadership in divorce proceedings. A wife could not claim a divorce from her husband. But a husband could denounce his wife.

When a man took a wife and it happened that she found no favor in his eyes because he found some indecency in her, he was to write her a certificate of divorce and puts it in her hand and sends her out from his house (Deut. 24:1). The Hebrew word ʿerwā (ערוה), derived from the verb ʿērā (ערה), is a legal term for improper behavior, usually related to a woman.[6] What is improper behavior for women has long been debated in Israel. In the

---

cubine. In that case, Gilimninu herself shall have authority over the offspring"(*HSS* 5[1929], No. 67; for a translation see *AASOR* 10 [1930]: 31 ff.; cf Speiser, *Genesis*, 120). Cf. Gen. 30:3-6.

5. Cf. Gen. 21:3; 22:23; 24:24,47; 25:3; 34:1; 41:50; 44:27; 46:15, 20 etc.

6. P. C. Craigie, *The Book of Deuteronomy* (NICOT; Grand Rapids: Eerdmans, 1976), 305.

Rabbinic period, the Shammai were so strict as in their interpretation of the text that they regarded adultery as the only case for divorce. However, the Hillel, who were liberal compared with the Shammai, set their own standards for divorce, and they could send their wives away at any time when they did not satisfy those standards. They could even divorce their wives in the case of poor cooking or being out of favor.[7]

We are not clear about the process of divorce in Israel. However, it can be reconstructed as follows. A husband might have pronounced the divorce. The divorce formula, as has been observed in the previous chapter, was "You are not my wife and I am not your husband"(Hos. 2:2), or simply "I am not your husband." The husband wrote a bill of divorce (ספר כריתות) for his wife and sent her out of his house. The divorced woman might have gone back to her father's house (Judg.19:2). This is obviously the opposite of marriage when the husband brings his wife to his house after the marriage contract. These common elements in marriage as well as divorce can be found in the ancient Near East. According to the Code of Hammurabi the husband proclaimed the divorce and wrote the divorce certificate.[8] In the code the amount of payment for a divorce was specified. However, it is not mentioned in the Bible.

5. THE REMARRIAGE IN ISRAEL

There are few examples of remarriage in the Bible. Perhaps the writ of divorce was a kind of document warranting the remarriage for the outcast woman. However, Deut. 24:2-4 draws attention to a case involving remarriage. If a woman once divorced got married to another man, and the latter husband also turned against her and wrote her a certificate of divorce and put it in her hand and sent her out of his house, or the latter husband died, then the former husband was not permitted to take her again for his wife because it was an abomination before YHWH. However, it is a riddle for scholars to decipher why it was an abomination. Some say that if it had been allowed, the respect for holy matrimony would be diminished and people would divorce very easily. Therefore, the purpose of this law was to protect

---

7. R. de Vaux, 35.
8. Cf. Ch.2. The Divorce Formula

marriage.[9] Others propose that this law came from putting a priority on the prohibition of marriage between close relatives. For the people of Israel, a marriage bound the couple to be a husband and wife as well as a brother and sister. Even though a divorce broke the husband and wife relationship, the brother and sister relationship was still maintained. Thus, if a divorced couple would be reunited, it would be a marriage between a brother and sister. This is condemned in the Bible.[10] Whatever reason there might be, it was an abomination before God, and it was prohibited.

As we survey marriage customs in Israel, we find that there was no big difference in its meaning and process as we have traced in the previous chapter. The husband took the initiative and leadership in the engagement, wedding, married life, divorce, and remarriage. The father handed over the ownership of his daughter to her husband. Engagement and marriage were regarded as legally the same. A marriage certificate was drawn up. Whereas the husband was to provide a domicile, clothing and food, the wife was to be faithful to her husband and give birth to a child, particularly an heir, for her husband. Divorce was permitted by writing a bill of divorce, but remarriage between the former couple was not permitted. A marriage in Israel carried the concept and character of a covenant, a covenant in which YHWH was involved.

---

9. P. C. Craigie, 305-6.
10. G. J. Wenham, *Genesis 1-15* (WBC 1; Waco: Word Books, 1987), 70-71.

CHAPTER IV

The Marriage between YHWH and Israel

In the previous chapter we have observed that the people of Israel employed their marriage terms, formulae, customs and concepts to understand and describe their relationship with YHWH. Now it is time for us to examine the YHWH-Israel relationship from the perspective of marriage. YHWH, as a husband, takes Israel as his wife. This marriage analogy begins at the engagement and runs through the wedding, married life, divorce, and remarriage. Therefore, it is necessary to investigate how each stage is portrayed on a theological level.

1. YHWH'S ENGAGEMENT TO ISRAEL

The exodus was the beginning of the YHWH-Israel relationship. At that time Israel was a slave of Pharaoh, the king of Egypt, and was oppressed by forced labor. The Egyptians made their lives bitter with a multitude of hard work in the house and field. They groaned in their slavery and cried out (Ex. 2:23) for deliverance. Furthermore, the king of Egypt issued a decree mandating birth control. He commanded the Hebrew midwives to kill any child at birth if it were a boy, but if it were a girl, the child was allowed to live (Ex. 1:15-16). Thus, the continuance of Israel as a nation was only a matter of time.

At this critical period YHWH went to Egypt to begin his work of deliverance. In Deut 4:34 it states, "Or has any god tried to go to take for himself (לבוא לקחת לו) a nation from within another nation by trials, by signs and wonders and by war and by a mighty hand and by outstretched arm and by great terrors as YHWH your God did for you in Egypt before your eyes?" Here YHWH is said "to go" (לבוא) and "to take for himself"(לו לקחת). These terms and expressions found in the marriage context are obviously reminiscent of a bridegroom going to the house of his bride to take her to his home. Furthermore, in Jer. 2:2 YHWH said,

> I remember concerning you the devotion of your youth,
> The love of your betrothals (כלולתיך),
> Your following after me in the wilderness,
> Through a land not sown.

Israel's following after YHWH in the wilderness is identified with the love of her betrothal. This phrase obviously refers to the exodus and her wondering in the wilderness of Sinai. In the following verse 6, a more reasonable basis for this interpretation is provided. The Hebrew noun, *kelûlot* (כלולת) means "engagement," or "the state of engagement." The expression of Israel following YHWH in the wilderness is compared to a girl following her fiance until their wedding during the period of engagement. This comparison seems to be intended to show that the exodus event signifies something more than the political deliverance from Egypt. The marriage term used here, *lāqaḥ* (לקח, to take), is one of the typical election terms used along with *bāḥar* (בחר) in the OT.[1] Election is an exclusive love relationship between YHWH and his people. YHWH initiates this relationship and we call this "election" in the narrow sense of the word. However, we need to expand the meaning of election to mean "an exclusive love relationship between YHWH and Israel."[2]

YHWH's election of Israel as his people is very similar to a man's selection of his wife in many aspects. In Ex. 6:6-7, YHWH says that he wants to take Israel as his people and he will be their God. YHWH expresses his will to establish a special relationship, as it were, an exclusive love relationship between God and his people.

> Say, therefore, to the sons of Israel, "I am YHWH and I will bring you out from under the burdens of the Egyptians, and I will deliver you from their

---

1. Seock-Tae Sohn, *The Divine Election of Israel*, 11-15.
2. Ibid., 4-5.

bondage. I will also redeem you with an outstretched arm and with great judgments. Then I will take you for my people, and I will be your God; and you shall know that I am YHWH your God, who brought you out from under the burdens of Egyptians." (Ex. 6:6-7)

YHWH delivers and redeems the people of Israel from under the bondage of the Egyptians in order to take them to be his people and establish a special relationship with them. Therefore, the exodus was YHWH's first step in this plan, and the exodus was a visible sign of YHWH's election of Israel as his people. The same idea can be found in Deut. 4:20, "But YHWH had taken you and brought you out of the iron furnace, from Egypt, to be a people for his own possession, as today." Deut. 7:6-7 also provides a theological relation between the exodus and election. Ex. 6:7; Deut. 4:20, 34; 7:6-8 are the key verses for the foundation of election theology as well as for the relation between YHWH's election of Israel and the exodus event. YHWH delivers Israel out of Egypt in order to have this special relationship. This is compared to a man going to a girl's house to take her as his wife and bring her into his house. The marriage term *lāqaḥ* (לקח) is here used as an election term and the marriage formula, "I will be your husband and you will be my wife," is used as an election formula. Thus, we can see that the exodus is described in terms of an engagement in which a groom takes his bride and brings her into his house for their wedding.

2. YHWH'S MARRIAGE TO ISRAEL

YHWH brought Israel to Mount Sinai after the exodus. There he made a covenant with them. He proposes the words of covenant through Moses as follows:

Thus you shall say to the house of Jacob and tell the sons of Israel: "You yourselves have seen what I did to the Egyptians, and how I bore you on eagle's wings, and brought you to myself. Now then, if you indeed obey my voice and keep my covenant, then you shall be my own possession among all the peoples, for all earth is mine; and you shall be a kingdom of priests and a holy nation." These are the words that you shall speak to the sons of Israel. (Ex. 19:4-6)

YHWH, THE HUSBAND OF ISRAEL

On the condition of obedience and adherence to the covenant, YHWH was about to take the Israelites for his own people, a kingdom of priests and a holy nation so as to become their God. This was agreeable to the people of Israel. Thus YHWH commanded Moses to assemble the people together on the mountain and made the covenant with them.

Ex. 24:1-8 describes the scene of this covenant more vividly. YHWH again proclaims the commandments and stipulations before making the covenant with Israel. The Israelites answered, "All the words which YHWH has spoken we will do." The people unanimously agreed. Oral agreement was established. Moses wrote down all the words of YHWH. He arose early in the morning and built an altar at the foot of the mountain with twelve pillars for the twelve tribes of Israel. There they sacrificed young bulls as offerings to YHWH. Moses took the book of the covenant and read it to the people and they replied again, "All that YHWH has spoken we will do, and we will be obedient" (Ex. 24:7). Then Moses took half of the blood and sprinkled it on the altar and the other half of it on the people and said, "Behold the blood of the covenant, which YHWH has made with you in accordance with all theses words"(8). YHWH made a blood covenant with Israel.

After this Moses went up to God with Aaron, Nadab, Abihu, and seventy of the elders of Israel and they ate and drank in his presence (Ex. 24:9-11). They took a covenant meal. We can see this type of practice in the case of Isaac's covenant with Abimelech (Gen. 26:26-34) and Jacob's covenant with Laban (Gen. 31:44-54) which was one of the important elements in making a covenant and was regarded as a covenant sign or seal.[3] This occasion was to celebrate the covenant and meant it would take effect from that point. Throughout this communion, YHWH did not stretch out his hand against the nobles of the sons of Israel (Ex. 24: 11). This is obviously contrasted with the scenes prior to making the covenant. At that time YHWH gave a strong warning to the people not to approach him on the mountain (Ex. 19: 7-25). YHWH met his people from a distance. However, no obstacle can be found here in their relationship; rather, perfect communion was established between them.

---

3. D. J. McCarthy says that this covenant meal is a symbol of the covenant, a sort of acted sign. "Three Covenants in Genesis," *CBQ* 26 (1964): 179-89.

One thing to be noted here is that the sprinkling of blood was used for both YHWH and Israel in making a covenant through Moses, the mediator. In ancient Semitic society it was very rare to use the blood of an animal on the covenant partners. In most cases, as we see in the covenant between YHWH and Abraham in Gen. 15, the covenant partners brought their animal and cut it into two pieces, laying each half opposite the other, and then the partners passed between those pieces. By this rite the covenant partners took an oath to be like the animal cut in two in the event that the covenant was broken. The animal was not necessarily to be cut in half. A donkey was killed in Mari, and the neck of a sheep was cut in Alalakh.[4] However, the basic purpose of the ritual was the same. They tried to secure the sincerity and faithfulness of the covenant and ensure a curse and retribution for the one who might break the covenant. Accordingly, there was no difference in the purpose and idea implied in the rite between sprinkling the blood of an animal on the covenant partners and passing through the pieces of the animal which has been cut in two or the slain body. Through this ceremony YHWH became the God of Israel and Israel became the people of YHWH. YHWH and Israel were legally bound together. The legal force was imposed on their relationship through this covenant. It is to be remembered that YHWH wanted to take Israel as his people in order to make them "his own possession among all the peoples" (Ex.19:5). Thus, YHWH proclaimed his ownership over Israel through this covenant. This is the reason why the people of Israel were called "my people" (*'ammî*, עמי), "my people of possession" (*'am segulā*, עם סגלה), and "my people of inheritance" (*'am naḥalā*, עם נחלה).[5] The main point of the Sinai covenant was for YHWH to take Israel as his own possession.

On the basis of the previous historical events, we are now to examine how the Biblical writers and the prophets of Israel understood the nature of this Sinai covenant and how they explained it. Jeremiah wrote:

---

4. Nahum Sarna, *Genesis: The JPS Torah Commentary* (Philadelphia: Jewish Publication Society, 1989), 114-15.

5. Though *'am segulā* (עם סגלה) and *'am naḥalā* (עם נחלה) are used interchangeably in the Bible, the origin and setting of these phrases seem to be different. *'am segulā* (עם סגלה) used in the context of marraige metaphor since a wife was usually a possession of husband. And *'am naḥalā* (עם נחלה) used in the father-son metaphor because a son was an heir of his father and inherited his father's property.

YHWH, THE HUSBAND OF ISRAEL

> "Behold, days are coming," declares YHWH, "when I will make a new covenant with the house of Israel and with the house of Judah, not like the covenant which I made with their fathers in the day I took them by the hand to bring them out of the land of Egypt, my covenant which they broke, although I was a husband to them," declares YHWH. "But this is the covenant which I will make with the house of Israel after those days," declares YHWH, "I will put my law within them, and on their heart I will write it; and I will be their God, and they shall be my people." (Jer. 31:31-33)

Jeremiah 31 prophesies the restoration of Israel during the exile and describes the relationship between YHWH and Israel in terms of various metaphors. YHWH calls Israel a "virgin" (v. 4, 21). In verse 9, YHWH employs father-son imagery to describe his relationship with Israel and in verse 20 he calls Ephraim "my dear son, a delightful child." In verse 10, YHWH is compared to a shepherd gathering his scattered sheep. In verse 27, YHWH is described as a farmer sowing seed and Israel as the seed. All these metaphors delineate the YHWH-Israel relationship after the restoration.

It is to be noted that verse 1 begins with the covenant formula: "I will be the God of all the families of Israel, and they shall be my people." We have already observed that this formula is a theological one borrowed from the marriage covenant. YHWH made a covenant with Israel at Mount Sinai. However, this covenant relationship was already broken at the time of Jeremiah. Thus, verse 1 is to be understood in the context of future restoration. Though this covenant basically retains the continuity with that of the Sinai covenant in terms of relationship, the content cannot be same. For this reason, Jeremiah uses the term "new covenant" in order to distinguish it from the old covenant and stresses the differences between them. The old covenant is the one that was made on the day YHWH took them by the hand to bring them out of the land of Egypt. It refers to the Sinai covenant. The expression "YHWH's taking Israel by the hand" reminds us of a man who takes a girl and brings her to his house in order to make her his wife. The new covenant will be different from the old one with respect to its durability, since the old one was broken, even though YHWH himself was their husband as the covenant partner. YHWH portrays himself as a husband at the time of making the old covenant at Sinai. The Hebrew term, *baʿal* (בעל) which means "a husband" or "a possessor," is used here.[6]

Jeremiah regards the Sinai covenant as a wedding ceremony between YHWH and Israel. It is natural for him to portray the covenant ceremony as a wedding since a marriage was a covenant, and a wedding was a kind of covenant ceremony in the ancient Near East. YHWH will not carve his law on a stone again; rather he will write it on the hearts of man and he will be their God and they will be his people (33). Then everyone will know him. It is very significant that the word *yādaʿ* (ידע), describing the most intimate relationship between a married couple, is used here. From this perspective the covenant meal that the seventy elders of Israel had in front of YHWH after making the covenant on the mount can be understood as a wedding feast.

Since marriage is a covenant, the married couple enters into a legal relationship through the wedding. Marriage legally binds the couple. Even though a man and woman cohabit together and have children without a wedding ceremony, their relationship is not acknowledged by their family and community and is not protected by law. Their children would be regarded as illegitimate. If the husband denounces her and casts her out of his house, the woman will not be able to claim her rights as a wife since she is no longer his wife. If they were a normal couple, a divorce case would have to be brought to court and the husband would write the divorce certificate and pay a certain amount of money for her. Thus, the marriage is an institution that carries legal, moral, and ethical forces.

It is from this perspective that the covenant between YHWH and Israel is to be understood. YHWH chose Israel from among many nations. The choice was from his sovereign and free will. He was pleased to choose Israel and

---

6. Bright and Thompson propose that the rendering of the phrase, "ואנכי בעלתי בם" as "Though I was their Lord" rather than "Though I was a husband to them." John Bright, *Jeremiah*, 283. J. A. Thompson, *The Book of Jeremiah* (NICOT; Grand Rapids: Eerdmans, 1980), 581n.2. However, the imagery of YHWH does not fit with that of God taking Israel by the hand and leading them out of Egypt. In this sentence the role of the conjunction *waw* (ו) cannot be ignored. Many commentators and translators prefer to regard it as having a concessional meaning of "though" or "although." However, the context leads us to read it from the perspective of time or the situation of making a covenant. Thus, "Then" would be more plausible as its translation. Jewish tradition also shows that the day that the Sinai covenant was made, the day that the Law was given, has been understood as the Day of the Espouser. Song of Songs R. 3.11.2. L. Ginsberg, *The Legends of the Jews* (Philadelphia: Jewish Publication Society, 1928), 6.36n. 200.

loved them (Deut. 4:37; 10:15; Isa. 41:8; 43:4; Mal. 1:2; Ps. 47:5; 78:68).[7] However, this kind of relationship was very weak and easy to be broken. It is a one-sided relationship without responsibility or legal force. As it were, a relationship without a covenant does not carry any legal force between the love partners. Likewise, in YHWH's election of Israel there is no responsibility or legal force without a covenant. YHWH may choose Israel and love her, but he may denounce her without any fair reason if he dislikes her. Thus, in election there is love only, but no legal ties binding the couple together. In the stage of election there is no law to punish Israel even though she betrayed and rebelled against YHWH.

However, YHWH made the covenant with Israel on the mountain of Sinai and he entered into a legal relationship with her. Through the covenant YHWH and Israel were bound together and share legal responsibility. YHWH was bound by Israel and Israel was equally bound. This does not mean that the authority and freedom of YHWH as the creator is limited by Israel; rather, YHWH has an exclusive love relationship with Israel. Israel is also supposed to know and serve YHWH only and become the people of his possession. A covenant enforces the legal power of election. Without election, there is no covenant. Election without a covenant brings a relationship without obligation and responsibility.

3. YHWH'S DWELLING WITH ISRAEL

YHWH chose Israel, the slave of Pharaoh the king of Egypt, from among many nations as his people and brought them to Mount Sinai and made a covenant with them. Jeremiah understood this covenant as a marriage between YHWH and Israel. Usually after a wedding ceremony the groom takes his bride into the tent he has prepared and begins his new life with his wife. He was obliged to provide all the necessary daily goods for her including food and clothes, and his wife was to bear a son as an heir. Then how does the Bible understand and explain the life of Israel in the land of Canaan as YHWH's covenant people?

The purpose of YHWH's deliverance of Israel from Egypt was to give

---

7. Sohn, 47-50.

them the land flowing with milk and honey as he promised to Abraham, their forefather (Gen. 15:18-21; Ex. 3:8, 17). After crossing the Red Sea the people of Israel praised YHWH, "In thy lovingkindness thou hast led the people whom thou hast redeemed; In thy strength thou hast guided them to thy holy habitation" (Ex. 15:13). "Thy holy habitation" obviously refers to the destination of his guidance, which is the land of his dwelling. YHWH was about to give this land to his people and settle them there. In this respect it is not a coincidence that *hōšîḇ* (השיב, to provide a domicile for a [woman]), the marriage term, is used for YHWH's settling of Israel in the land of Canaan. Thus, YHWH's settling of Israel in the land of Canaan can be compared to a husband's taking of his bride and providing a domicile for her. Thus Canaan is understood as a "resting place"(מנוח) for Israel in Dt. 12:9; 1Kgs 8:56; Is. 11:18.

Another purpose for YHWH's deliverance of Israel out of Egypt can be found in his commandment to build the tabernacle "in order to dwell among them."

> "And I will dwell among the sons of Israel and will be their God, and they shall know that I am YHWH their God who brought them out of the land of Egypt, that I might dwell among them; I am YHWH their God." (Ex. 29:45-46)

YHWH as the God of Israel wanted to dwell among them and continue the covenant relationship with them. The tabernacle was a symbol, as well as a reality, that YHWH dwelt among his covenant people. Lev. 26:11,12 states, "Moreover, I will make my dwelling among you and my soul will not reject you. I will also walk among you and be your God and you shall be my people." This clearly shows that the tabernacle's presence among the people of Israel was a visible sign of YHWH's dwelling among his people and a symbol of the covenant relationship between them. Ex. 40:34-38 describes YHWH's glorious appearance in the tabernacle after it was made.

> Then the cloud covered the tent of meeting and the glory of YHWH filled the tabernacle. And Moses was not able to enter the tent of meeting because the cloud had settled on it and the glory of YHWH filled the tabernacle. And throughout all their journeys whenever the cloud was taken up from over the tabernacle, the sons of Israel would set out; but if the cloud was not taken up, then they did not set out until the day when it was taken up. For throughout all their journeys, the cloud of YHWH was on the tabernacle by day, and

there was fire in it by night, in the sight of all the house of Israel. (Ex. 40:34-38)

The presence of YHWH, portrayed by cloud and fire, settled on the tent of meeting day and night and led the people of Israel throughout all their journeys to Canaan. Num. 9:15-23 emphasizes that the presence of YHWH was always with the people in the form of a cloud during the day and fire during the night (cf. 10:33-34; Deut. 1:33). We can also observe YHWH's dwelling among the people of Israel in the mode of Israel's pitching of tents in the wilderness. The sons of Israel camped around the tent of meeting (Num. 2:1). On the east side of the tent of meeting camped Judah, Issachar, and Zebulun (Num. 2:3-9). On the south side come the tribes of Reuben, Simeon, and Gad (Num. 2:10-17). On the west side comes the tribes of Ephraim, Manasseh, and Benjamin (2:18-24). And the tribes of Dan, Asher, and Naphtali camped on the north side of the tent. Therefore, YHWH's tent always comes in the center of Israel's camp. Of course this camp formation is designed for the battle, and it also signifies YHWH's dwelling among his people. YHWH's dwelling among the people of Israel is parallel to their custom of marriage. A man and woman dwell together after marriage; likewise, YHWH dwells among his people.

Not only does YHWH dwell among his people, but he also provides his people with everything that is necessary for their living. This is similar to the case of a husband who provides the domicile, food and clothes for his wife and protects her. Lev. 26:1-3 describes YHWH's basic responsibility for Israel as the Lord of the covenant. He will send rain in its season, and let the ground yield its crops and the trees of the field their fruits (5-6). Before they consume the last year's harvest, they will have a new one (10). YHWH promised them an abundance of food. Verses 6-8 are a description of a promise concerning their security. The threat to his people would be the wild animals as well as the gentile enemy attacking from the outside. Against this kind of attack, he promised his protection and peace for his people so that his people would multiply and be prosperous. These are the responsibilities of YHWH dwelling among Israel.

Until now we have observed the responsibility of YHWH for Israel, his covenant people. What then is Israel's responsibility to their covenant Lord, YHWH? In the Decalogue, YHWH requires Israel to have no other gods before him (Ex. 20:3) because he is YHWH their God who brought them out of the land of Egypt, out of the house of slavery (Ex. 20:2). This is the first commandment out of ten which he required of his people as he made a covenant with them. This is similar to a husband who requires fidelity from his wife as he takes her as his spouse. In Ex. 20:5 YHWH introduces himself as jealousy itself by saying, "I, YHWH your God, am a jealous God" (אנכי יהוה אלהיך אל קנא). In Deut. 4:24 YHWH is called a "consuming fire" (אש אכלה) in relation to his character of jealousy. Again in Deut. 29:20 YHWH says that his anger and jealousy will burn against the apostates. These expressions are used in the context of warning against Israel's rebellion. YHWH's jealousy will burn like a fire when Israel worships the gods of other nations and serves them. This kind of jealousy is obviously a result of YHWH's ardent love for his people, Israel.

YHWH required his covenant people to be separated from her neighbors. YHWH separated Israel from all the nations of the world to be his people. Deut. 14:2 shows the relationship between being the chosen people and a holy people. "For you are a holy people to YHWH your God; and YHWH has chosen you to be a people for his own possession out of all the peoples who are on the face of the earth." According to this verse, the people of Israel are his holy people (עם קדוש) because YHWH has chosen (בחר) them as his own possession. The term, "holy people" (עם קדוש) is a theological term denoting the idea of election such as "a people of inheritance" (עם נחלה) or "a people of possession" (עם סגלה). A word study shows that *qādaš* (קדש), the verb form of *qādoš* (קדוש), means "to set apart." Accordingly, *qādoš* (קדוש) carries the primary meaning of "separation" or "distinction" rather than ritual holiness, even though it is usually translated as "holy." Holiness is to keep "separated" what YHWH has separated and to maintain the distinctions he has enumerated. Therefore, YHWH says of himself "I am YHWH who sanctify you" (אני יהוה מקדשכם, Lev. 22: 32). He commands, "Thus you are to be holy to me, for I, YHWH, am holy; and I have set you apart from the peoples to be mine." (Lev. 20:26).

Then where can this separatedness be found? Israel had to show their difference from their neighbors in every area of their life including religion, morality, ethics, politics, economy, and even in war, etc. Moreover, they had to manifest that they were the people of YHWH, possessed by him. The basic principle and foundation of the law that YHWH had given to Israel was holiness and separatedness. If Israel did not conform to the lifestyle of the neighboring nations, she would be the true people of YHWH. But if they married gentiles and served other gods and followed their customs, Israel would lose the distinction of being YHWH's people. The people of Israel were called and chosen to do righteousness and justice (Gen. 18:19). They were obliged to be faithful to YHWH and to keep his commandments as his covenant people. They had to worship and serve only YHWH because they were his bride.

4. YHWH'S DIVORCE FROM ISRAEL

YHWH delivered Israel from the bondage of Egypt and he made her his people and he became her God by making a covenant with her at Mount Sinai. Thus, Israel had to serve only YHWH and live a life of holiness and a life of separation from her neighbors. Unfortunately, Israel did not keep her purity. Immediately after the covenant at Mount Sinai, they made a molten calf and worshiped it and sacrificed to it (Ex. 32). They worshiped other gods and followed the gentile customs and practices. They broke their covenant with YHWH. He had to curse and punish them according to the terms of the covenant. Deut. 29:22-29 describes a dialogue between them in case of further treachery against YHWH in the future.

> "Now the generation to come, your sons who rise up after you and the foreigner who comes from a distant land, when they see the plagues of the land and the diseases with which YHWH has afflicted it, will say, 'All its land is brimstone and salt, a burning waste, unsown and unproductive, and no grass grows in it, like the overthrow of Sodom and Gomorrah, Admah and Zeboiim, which YHWH overthrew in his anger and in His wrath.' "And all the nations shall say, 'Why has YHWH done thus to this land? Why this great outburst of anger?'" Then men shall say, 'Because they forsook the covenant of YHWH, the God of their fathers, which he made with them when he brought them out of the land of Egypt. And they went and served other gods and worshiped them, gods whom they have not known and whom he had not allotted to them. Therefore, the anger of YHWH burned against that land, to bring upon it every curse which is written in this book; and YHWH uprooted them from their land in anger and in fury and in great wrath, and

cast them into another land, as it is this day.' "The secret things belong to YHWH our God, but the things revealed belong to us and to our sons forever, that we may observe all the words of this law." (Deut. 29:22-29)

The reason for YHWH's anger and Israel's humiliation is that the Israelites, forsaking the covenant of YHWH, went and served other gods and worshiped them. The main point of YHWH's curse was to uproot his people from their land and cast them into another land. The terms such as "to sow"(נטע, שׁתל), "to uproot"(נתשׁ) and "to cast"(שׁלך) represent the idea of election and rejection.[8] YHWH, who brought Israel out of the land of Egypt and settled them in the land of Canaan, is compared to the farmer of a vineyard who planted a vine on the land, whereas the imagery of a farmer uprooting the vine describes YHWH's curse on the people who were taken captive into the land of Assyria and Babylon because they broke their covenant with him. YHWH's taking them away from the land and casting them into another land was his punishment on his people who worshiped and served other gods.

Then, how does the Bible explain YHWH's punishment of the rebellious Israelites in terms of the theme of marriage? YHWH says that his people played the harlot. He uses the same language and inflicts the same punishment that a husband uses for an adulterous wife. The people of Israel were not to worship or serve other gods since they were the covenant people of YHWH. However, they made the molten calf while Moses went up the mountain to receive the Commandments, and they called the calf their god who brought them up from the land of Egypt. They even offered burnt offerings to the idol and brought peace offerings to it, and the people sat down to eat and drink and rose up to play. YHWH was angry and punished them without mercy (Ex. 32). YHWH commanded Israel not to make any covenant with the inhabitants of the land of Canaan and not to worship any other gods besides him because they played the harlot with their gods (Ex. 34:15-17). The Hebrew term *zānā* (זנה) carries the meaning of "to play the harlot" describing the activities of prostitutes. In a metaphorical sense, it also describes Israel's worship and service to other gods. The prophets of Israel employed the terms and images of a whore in order to describe Israel's immorality and rebellion against YHWH.

"You are not my people and I am not your God"(אתם לא עמי ואנוכי

---

8. Sohn, 80-84; 212-13.

YHWH, THE HUSBAND OF ISRAEL

לא־אלהיכם, Hos. 1:9) was the formula YHWH had to pronounce against his rebellious people.[9] This is obviously modified from the divorce formula: "You are not my wife and I am not your husband" (היא לא אשתי ואנכי לא אשה) as we see in Hos. 2:4 (E. 2:2).[10] YHWH took the initiative to reject Israel as a husband did against his wife at the time of his divorce. We can find many other expressions and descriptions to represent the concept of divorce in the Bible.

(1) YHWH Writes a Certificate of Divorce

In Deut. 24:1, when a wife finds no favor in her husband's eyes due to some indecency he has found in her, the husband is permitted to write her a bill of divorce (ספר כריתת). In the same way, YHWH says that he has written a bill of divorce and has given it to Israel.

> And I saw that for all the adulteries of faithless Israel, I had sent her away and given her a writ of divorce, yet her treacherous sister Judah did not fear, but she went and was a harlot also. (Jer. 3:8)

When YHWH made a covenant with Israel on Mount Sinai, he gave the two tablets as a marriage certificate. Now he has sent her away and given her a divorce certificate because she was not faithful to YHWH, her husband, but has served other gods. The phrase: "to send her away" obviously referred to the exile of the northern kingdom to Assyria and the southern kingdom to Ba-

---

9. MT reads אליכם instead of אהיה־לכם. However, it would be more proper to follow the reading of *BHS* since it is a divorce formula.

10. The divorce formula, "You are not my wife," "You are not my husband" can be found in Old Babylonian marriage documents. See Rivkah Harris, "The Case of Three Babylonian Marriage Contracts," *JNES* 33/4 (October, 1974): 363-69. In the Elephantine text, divorce, whether by husband or by wife, is effected by the utterance of the proper formula. The husband says, "I divorce X my wife" (*BMAP*, 2:7, 143; *BAP*, 15:27, 46); *BMAP*, 7:21-22, 205, adds, "She shall not be to me a wife." The wife, if the divorce is by her initiative, says, "I divorce X my husband" (*BMAP*, 2:9, 143; *BAP* 15:23, 46). The formula in *BMAP*, 7:25, 207, is, "I divorce thee, I will not be to thee a wife." See Reuven Yaron, "Aramaic Marriage Contracts from Elephantine," *JSS* 3/1 (1958): 14.

bylon. The same expression is found in Isa. 50:1.

> Thus says YHWH,
> "Where is the certificate of divorce
> by which I have sent your mother away?
> Or to whom of my creditors did I sell you?
> Behold you are sold for your iniquities
> And for your transgression your mother was sent away."

In this verse "your mother" refers to the ancestors of Israel during the period of the exile. The reason YHWH sent her away and sold her to her creditors was her iniquities and transgressions. We can see here that YHWH wrote a marriage document on the tablets at the time the covenant was made with Israel on Mount Sinai, and he wrote a certificate of divorce at the time of their rejection when they were sent away as Assyrian and Babylonian captives.

(2) YHWH Sends Israel out of His House

When a man took a woman to be his wife, he was to go and take her into his house and provide a domicile for her. Likewise, YHWH, the husband of Israel, went to Egypt (Deut. 4:34) and brought her out, providing her with the land of Canaan as her dwelling place. Since divorce is the opposite of marriage, the phrase, "to send out from the house" (שלחה מביתו) is used in contrast to the phrase, "to provide a domicile" (Deut. 22:19, 29; 24:1,3,4). In the same way the Hebrew bible employs the expression of "sending out from the house" as a sign of YHWH's rejection of Israel. In Jer. 3:8, YHWH said that he had sent Israel out and given her a writ of divorce. YHWH warned his people that they would be sent away from his presence and that he would let them go in Jer. 15:1 (cf. Is. 50:1).

As a rough expression for this idea, $gāla\check{s}$ (גלש) is sometimes used. It means "to banish," or "to drive out." $Gerûšā$ (גלושה), the Qal passive participle of $gāla\check{s}$ (גלש), is used for "a divorced woman" or "widow" (Lev. 21:7, 14; 22:13; Num. 30:10 [E.9]). When this verb is used in reference to YHWH, in most cases it refers to his driving out the nations from the land of Canaan for Israel (Ex. 6:1; 23:30; 33:2; Num. 22:6; Josh. 24:18; Judg. 2:3; Ps. 78:55). However, it is also used for YHWH's driving Israel out of his house.

YHWH, THE HUSBAND OF ISRAEL

> All their evils at Gilgal;
> Indeed, I came to hate them there!
> Because of the wickedness of their deeds
> I will drive them out of my house!
> I will love them no more;
> All their princes are rebels. (Hos. 9:15)

In relation to the concept of "sending out from the house," we can think of "going back to her father's house" (אבה הלך ושוב לבית). Since she was taken from her father's house, she was to go back to the place where she belonged when she was rejected by her husband, or when the marriage bond was no longer effective. Thus, Naomi's two daughters-in-law were told: "Go, return each of you to her mother's house"(Ruth 1:8). This same expression is employed for YHWH's rejection of Israel. YHWH warned his people that they would be sent back to Egypt in case of their disobedience.

> If you are not careful to observe all the words of this law which are written in this book, to fear this honored and awesome name, YHWH your God. . . . And it shall come about that as YHWH delighted over you to prosper you, and multiply you, so YHWH will delight over you to make you perish and destroy you; and you shall be torn from the land where you are entering to possess it. . . . And YHWH will bring you back to Egypt in ships, by the way about which I spoke to you, "You will never see it again! And there you shall offer yourselves for sale to your enemies as male and female slaves, but there will be no buyer." (Deut. 28:58-68)

YHWH is going to bring them back to Egypt and sell them as slaves when his people betray him. Hos. 8:18 and 9:3 also refer to YHWH's sending Israel away to Egypt because of their adulterous behavior.

> They will not remain in YHWH's land,
> But Ephraim will return to Egypt,
> And in Assyria they will eat unclean food. (Hos. 9:3)

Since the marriage bond between YHWH and Israel was broken because Israel played the harlot, Israel was to return to the place whence she was first taken and to the status of slave (cf. Hos. 8:13; 9:1; 11:5). At that time YHWH would put his hook in her nose and his bridle in her lips, and he

(3) YHWH Strips Israel

The placing of a garment over a woman is regarded as a symbolic claim to marriage. When Ruth went down to Boas' threshing floor and asked him to spread his covering over her (Ruth 3:9), it seemed to mean that she was making a request for marriage or sexual relations.[11] The same expression is directly used for the relationship between YHWH and Israel.

> "Then I passed by you and saw you, and behold, you were at the time for love; So I spread my skirt over you and covered your nakedness (אפרש כנפי עליך ואכסה ערותך). I also swore to you and entered into a covenant with you so that you became mine," declares YHWH God. (Ezek. 16:8)

This is a metaphor describing YHWH's taking Israel as his bride. YHWH said that he spread his skirt over her and covered her nakedness. It was obviously an important procedure for a man to spread his skirt and cover a woman in order to enter into a marriage relation.[12] Accordingly, the concept of "to strip"(פשט) is used for divorce, whereas the opposite term, "to cover" (כסה) is used for marriage. YHWH's stripping the skirts off over the face of Israel and leaving her naked and bare is a metaphorical expression of his rejection of her as his people.

> "This is your lot, the portion measured to you from me," declares YHWH, because you have forgotten me and trusted in falsehood. So I myself have also stripped your skirts off over your face, that your shame may be seen. As for your adulteries and your lustful neighings, the lewdness of your prostitution on the hills in the field, I have seen your abominations. Woe to you, O Jerusalem! How long will you remain unclean? (Jer. 13:25-27)

Here Israel's worship of idols on the hills in the field is described as an act of adultery and YHWH's stripping off their skirts is his corresponding reaction.

---

11. Edward F. Campbell, Jr. *Ruth* (AB; Garden City: Double-day & Company, 1978), 123.
12. Cf. Ch.2. 1.

YHWH, THE HUSBAND OF ISRAEL

Similar expressions can be found in Ezekiel (16:37, 39; 23:10, 26) and Hosea (2:3 [Heb. 5]).

(4) YHWH Forsakes Israel

Isa. 54:6 describes the rejected Israel as a wife forsaken (עזובה) and rejected (תמאס) in her youth.

> "For YHWH has called you,
> Like a wife forsaken (עזובה) and grieved in spirit,
> Even like a wife of one's youth when she is rejected (תמאס)" says your God.
> (Isa. 54:6)

In the context of YHWH's promise of deliverance from the Babylonian captivity, he compares himself to a husband who has forsaken his wife and Israel to a rejected wife. Thus, we can see here that the terms *ʿazûbā* (עזובה) and *māʾas* (מאס) are used in the field of divorce. Since YHWH was to forsake Israel, she would be called by the name "forsaken" (עזובה, Isa. 62:4). As for *māʾas* (מאס), Jer. 4:30 gives a perfect illustration of the rejected Israel.

> And you, O desolate one, what will you do?
> Although your dress is scarlet,
> Although you decorate yourself with ornaments of gold,
> Although you enlarge your eyes with paint,
> In vain you make yourself beautiful;
> Your lovers despise you (מאסו־כם);
> They seek your life.

In Jer. 6:30, even though the imagery is different from that of divorce, "rejected silver"(כסף נמאס) is used for a rejected Israel, because "YHWH has rejected them"(כי־מאס יהוה בהם).

(5) YHWH Forgets Israel

The Marriage between YHWH and Israel

In relation to the concept of YHWH's rejection of Israel, *zākar* (זכר, to remember) and *šakaḥ* (שׁכח, to forget) are noteworthy. These terms are not directly related to a description of marriage or divorce. Whereas *zākar* (זכר, to remember) denotes the attitude of kindness toward others, *šakaḥ* (שׁכח, to forget) is to show intentional coldness and indifference. When the term *šakaḥ* (שׁכח) is used between spouses, it describes the status of their broken relationship (Prov.2:17; Jer.30:14). They remember nothing about each other, and even love and hatred toward their partners are erased. Thus, the term *šakaḥ* (שׁכח, to forget) is one of the metaphorical terms denoting the idea of rejection. Particularly, it is used as a divorce term for a married couple.

The term *šakaḥ* (שׁכח, to forget) is used for YHWH in response to Israel's forgetting him (Isa. 49:14; Hos. 4:6).

> Yet I have been YHWH your God
> Since the land of Egypt;
> And you were not to know any god except me,
> For there is no savior besides me.
> I cared for you (ידעתיך) in the wilderness,
> In the land of drought.
> As they had their pasture, they became satisfied,
> And being satisfied, their heart became proud;
> Therefore, they forgot me (שׁכחוני). (Hos. 13:4-6)

From the time of the exodus, Israel had a special relationship with YHWH. He had specially cared for Israel. It should be remembered that *yāḏaʿ* (ידע), translated here as "cared for," is a marriage term. And if we remember that the image of pasturing and satisfying describe the obligation of a husband for his wife, these words of YHWH are easily understood to be spoken as a husband to his wife, Israel. Israel forgot YHWH as they became satisfied. In Hos. 2:13 (Heb. 15) YHWH said that Israel followed her lover and forgot him. Since Israel forgot him (Jer. 2:32; 3:21; 18:15; Ezek. 22:12; Isa. 51:13), YHWH also forsook and forgot her (Hos. 4:6; Isa. 49:14).

In addition to the above examples, the negative counterpart to "YHWH's loving Israel" is found in the phrases: "I set my face against them" (נתתי את־פני בהם, Jer. 21:10; 44:11, 27; Ezek. 14:8; 15:7; Amos 9:4) and "I have hidden my face" (הסתרתי פני, Jer. 33:5; Isa. 54:8).

As we have seen, YHWH wrote a certificate of divorce and gave it to

Israel, and he stripped her of her garments and exposed her nakedness; he forsook and forgot her. Obviously these images are borrowed from the practice of human divorce. The series of historical events such as Israel's breaking his covenant and being cast out of Canaan and her Babylonian captivities, etc. are delineated in terms of the metaphor of YHWH's divorce of Israel. As covenant making was portrayed in terms of the imagery of marriage, covenant breaking was portrayed in terms of the imagery of divorce. Particularly, it is very significant that YHWH's rejection of Israel as his chosen nation and the subsequent fall of Israel are described through the metaphor of divorce.

5. YHWH'S REMARRIAGE TO ISRAEL

Even though YHWH rejected Israel and sent her away because of her adultery, he could not stop loving her. His rejection was not permanent. He cries, "How can I give you up, O Ephraim? How can I surrender you, O Israel?" (Hos. 11:8). Though YHWH once rejected her, he could not forget her. Thus, YHWH is going to allure her (מפתיה) and bring her back to him (Hos. 2:16[E. 14]). Particularly, Isaiah 54:7-8 provides important concepts and images depicting the reunion of YHWH with Israel.

> "Fear not, for you shall not be put to shame;
> Neither feel humiliated, for you will not be disgraced;
> But you will forget the shame of your youth,
> And the reproach of your widowhood you will remember no more.
> "For your husband is your maker,
> Whose name is YHWH of hosts;
> And your redeemer is the holy one of Israel,
> Who is called the God of all the earth.
> "For YHWH had called you,
> Like a wife forsaken and grieved (עזובה ועצובת) in spirit,
> Even like a wife of one's youth when she is rejected (תמאס),"
> Says YHWH.
> "For a brief moment (ברגע קטן) I forsook you,
> But with great compassion I will gather you.
> "In an outburst of anger
> I hid my face from you for a moment;

The Marriage between YHWH and Israel

> But with everlasting lovingkindness
> I will have compassion on you"
> Says YHWH your redeemer. (Isa. 54:4-8)

YHWH, here, represents himself as the Lord of hosts, the creator of Israel, the holy one of Israel, redeemer, and the God of all the land, etc. He introduces himself as the husband (בעל) in relation to the theme of remarriage. However, as for Israel being referred to Zion here, he compares her to a forsaken and rejected wife in her youth. Accordingly, she is called "a wife forsaken and grieved in spirit and a wife of one's youth when she is rejected." YHWH and Israel in this context are described as a couple who have passed through the stages of marriage and divorce. Furthermore, YHWH attempts a reunion with his wife, Israel, and comforts her with great compassion. The phrases: "for a brief moment (ברגע קטן) I forsook you" and "I hid my face from you for a moment" show that YHWH's rejection was not a permanent one. It is now time to restore the relationship. In Isa. 62:4, YHWH says to Zion:

> "It will no longer be said to you, "Forsaken" (עזובה),
> Nor to your land will it any longer be said, "Desolate" (שממה);
> But you will be called, "My delight is in her" (חפצי־בה),
> And your land, "Married" (בעולה);
> For YHWH delights (חפץ) in you,
> And to him your land will be married (תבעל). (Isa. 62:4)

YHWH is going to dwell again in the desolate land. He describes himself here as a husband and bridegroom, and the city refers ultimately to Israel as his wife and bride.

Hos. 2:16-25(E. 14-23) gives a more vivid description of this reunion. On the day of restoration, YHWH will engage (ארש) himself to Israel forever (לעולם) (Hos. 2:21-22 [E. 19-20]). Here, $l^{e‘}ôlam$ (לעולם, forever) is noteworthy. Since the YHWH-Israel union was once broken, this word emphasizes the permanent, unchanging, and unbroken character of the union. Again YHWH will engage himself to Israel in righteousness (בצדק), in justice(במשפט), in lovingkindness(בחסד), in compassion (ברחמים), and in faithfulness (באמונה). These characteristics of reunion can hardly be found in a broken relationship. Of course YHWH showed these virtues in the first union. However, in these circumstances those kinds of virtues were needed for Israel more than any other times. YHWH was about to reunite himself with Israel with such virtues as those mentioned above. At this point YHWH asked to be called *Ishi* (אשי, my husband) rather than *Baali* (בעלי, my husband). Once a couple got married, the wife was to call her husband either Ishi or Baali. However, *Baali* (my husband) is a homonym of *Baali* (my Baal), the gods of Canaan, the lover of Israel with whom she played the harlot. Thus, YHWH asks her to call him *Ishi* (אשי) in order that he may remove the names of Baal from her mouth and that she would mention their names no more. The YHWH-Israel reunion reaches its climax in the proclamation of the marriage oath sworn by both parties as in the case of human marriage. The phrase, "You are my people, Thou art my God" (23 [Heb. 25]) is regarded as a modification of the marriage declaration, "You are my wife, you are my husband." In one aspect, this process of reunion is more formal and detailed than the first union. [13]

This renewed relationship is not without legal force. The bond of reunion has to be stronger and more permanent in its character than the first one so that it may not be broken or nullified again. The new covenant of Jer. 31:31-34 must be understood from this perspective of reunion. On the day of restoration, YHWH will make a new covenant with Israel which will be entirely different from the old one that was made on Mount Sinai with their fathers. At that time YHWH will not write the covenant document on stone but on their hearts so that it may not be broken. And he will proclaim, "I will be their God, and they shall be my people" (33). Thus, there will be no need to teach each other because everyone will know him personally. Here we can see the covenant formula (I will be their God, and they will be my people) modified from the marriage formula as an aspect of the new covenant. The

---

13. R. Yaron proposed the possibility of a second marriage after divorce in ancient Israel and asserted that Duet. 24:1-4 is a device to ensure its stability and continuation. See Yaron, "The Restoration of Marriage," *JJS* 17 (1966): 1-11. Though G. J. Wenham does not deny the practice of remarriage, he proposes a different reason for the prohibition of reunion between a divorced couple in Duet. 24:1-4. According to him, marriage establishes a close and lasting relationship between a woman and her husband's family, a relationship that survives divorce or the death of one of the parties. In marriage a woman became a part of her husband's family, a sister to him and his brother. Thus, if a divorced couple wanted to come together again, it would be as bad as a man marrying his sister. See Wenahm, "The Restoration of Marriage Reconsidered," *JJS* 29 (1978): 36-40.

new covenant is also viewed as a marriage treaty. These facts lead to the conclusion that even the new covenant is portrayed in terms of the marriage metaphor, and thus the legal bond of marriage through the new covenant is also one of the important parts of the YHWH-Israel reunion. This new covenant also has a basic continuity with the old one (cf. Ezek. 16:60). In Jer. 50:5, this covenant of reunion is named "an everlasting covenant"(ברית עולם), and in Ezek 37:26 it is identified with "the covenant of peace" (ברית שלום). Since the restoration metaphor carries the meaning of a marriage reunion, phrases such as "YHWH's making Israel live in its tents again"(Hos. 12:9), "YHWH's dwelling in the midst of Israel forever" (Ezek. 43:9; Joel 2:27), and "My dwelling place also will be with them; and I will be their God, and they will be my people" (Ezek. 37:27) are noteworthy. The reunion of YHWH-Israel is described in terms of the metaphors of a marriage reunion.

As has been observed, the YHWH-Israel relationship is portrayed through the marriage metaphor. The series of events related to marriage such as engagement, wedding, married life, divorce, and remarriage etc. are employed to described the YHWH-Israel's relationship such as election, covenant, covenant life, rejection, restoration, etc. It is significant that the YHWH-Israel relationship is understood from the perspective of a husband-wife relationship, which is the most intimate and personal one. Furthermore, it gives a special meaning to the nature of the relationship between YHWH and his people for the history of Israel from the exodus to the return from exile to be compared to a couple's life.

CHAPTER V

The Marriage Texts

We have observed that the people of Israel borrowed the imagery of a human marriage in order to explain their relationship with YHWH. The basic themes of Old Testament theology such as election, covenant, the life of the covenant people, rejection, and restoration are described in terms of the words, phrases and metaphors of engagement, wedding, married life, divorce, and re-marriage. Marriage between a man and woman is one of the most intimate human relationships and it cannot be compared with any other one. This relationship carries legal force and requires moral and ethical responsibility. Furthermore, this relationship is such a mysterious one that it is not easy to get a full logical explanation of its nature. However, it is our task to expound the biblical texts that describe the YHWH-Israel relationship through the marriage metaphor and expose the mysterious nature of it.

1. THE BOOK OF HOSEA 1-3

Hosea employs his tragic marital relationship to describe Israe's unfaithfulness to their covenant with YHWH. He portrays YHWH as a loving husband and Israel as an adulterous wife who has betrayed her husband. Hosea 1-3 seems to be lacking in unity and consistency on the surface. However, a close examination shows that there is organic unity and an inseparable relationship between the chapters. Following is an outline of Hos. 1-3.

    (1) Hosea's time (1:1)
    (2) Hosea and Gomer (1:2-9)

YHWH, THE HUSBAND OF ISRAEL

(3) YHWH and Israel (1:10-2:23)
(4) Hosea and YHWH (3:1-5)

Hos.1:1 mentions the date of the prophet's activity as an introduction. 1:2 presents Hosea's marriage to Gomer and the names of their children. Jezreel, Lo-ruhamah, and Lo-ammi are symbolic names prophesying the fate of Israel. 1:10-2:23 is a metaphor of Israel's disloyalty to YHWH, her husband. YHWH compares the adulterous Israel who followed Baal, the gods of Canaan, with the woman who betrayed her husband and followed her lover. Here YHWH rejected Israel as his people and later he restores them again to be his wife/people. In this context YHWH and Israel are portrayed as a married couple. 3:1-5 is the story of Hosea buying back his wife again according to the commandment of YHWH. This is a symbolic vision of YHWH who is about to restore Israel by paying the price for her adultery. Thus, Hos. 1-3 obviously contains unity in its content and description. It describes YHWH-Israel's relationship in terms of the marriage metaphor of a husband and wife.

(1) Hosea and His Time (Hos.1:1)

Hosea's prophetic ministry covered the days of Uzziah, Jotham, Ahaz, and Hezekiah, kings of Judah and the days of Jeroboam the son of Joash, king of Israel.[1] In this period Palestine experienced unprecedented political turmoil, the nations became involved in warfare, and international power structures were being reshuffled. In particular, Israel collapsed under the attack by Assyria and Judah also shared the same fate spiritually because of her apostasy.

We can see the most serious apostasy of Israel against YHWH in the days of Ahaz. This is because the religion of the ancient Near East was closely associated with politics. The pro-Assyrian inclination of Ahaz, king of Judah, began with the reaction of the Syro-Ephramite coalition against Assyria. In

---

1. Hosea's prophetic ministry seems to begin before the death of Jeroboam II of Israel (746 B.C.) and extends to the time after the accession of Hezekiah, king of Judah (715 B.C.). See James Ward, "The Message of the Prophet Hosea," *Interpretation*, 23/4 (1969): 388.

order to escape the allied forces of Rezin king of Syria and Pekah king of Israel, Ahaz sought military aid from Tiglath-pileser the king Assyria by offering him silver and gold which was taken from the temple and palace (2Kgs. 16:5-9). Due in part to this tribute, Ahaz could survive the calamity that overtook Israel, although Judah still became a vassal state of the Assyrian empire. According to ancient Near Eastern custom, Ahaz, as a vassal king, had to recognize his suzerain's gods and follow his directions. He went to Damascus and paid homage to the Assyrian gods at a bronze altar that stood there. While staying there, he made a copy of the altar that was sent to Urijah the priest to build according to its pattern and model. Thus, a new altar was erected in the temple, and the bronze altar which was before YHWH was set aside. When he returned from Damascus, he himself cut off the borders of the stands and removed the laver from there (16:7). He also ordered the periodic offering of various kinds of sacrifices according to the custom of Assyria (16:15). Thus the temple of YHWH was thoroughly desecrated. According to Bright:

> Since Ahaz was, as all the evidence indicates, without real faith in or zeal for the national religion, he did not exert himself to keep the defenses against paganism otherwise intact. As II Kings 16:3 f. alleges and as contemporary prophetic passages (e.g., Isa. 2:6-8, 20; 8:19f.; Mic. 5:12-14) indicate, native pagan practices flourished, together with all sorts of foreign fashions, cults, and superstitions. Ahaz is even charged, on what occasion we do not know, with offering his own son as a sacrifice in fulfillment of some vow or pledge, in accordance with contemporary pagan practice. The reign of Ahaz was remembered by later generations as one of the worst periods of apostasy that Judah had ever known.[2]

In this same period, the northern kingdom departed from YHWH and the entire nation fell into paganism. Furthermore, the continuous power struggle in the royal court weakened the country. Soon after the reign of Jeroboam II, we see the fall of Samaria and its consequent deportation into Assyria. When Ahaz asked for military aid from Assyria to defend himself against the attack of the Syro-Ephramite coalition, Tiglath-pileser the king Assyria came and occupied almost all the cities of Israel except for Samaria, the capital city. As a result of this defeat, Samaria became a vassal of Assyria. However, Hosea, the successor of Pekiah revolted against Shalmanezer V. This caused the

2. John Bright, *A History of Israel*, 275.

YHWH, THE HUSBAND OF ISRAEL

Assyrian invasion in 724 B.C. and the fall of Israel two years later in 722 B.C. (2 Kgs. 17:1-41). Therefore, both kingdoms faced critical situations politically as well as religiously. It was in these circumtances that Hosea's ministry began in the northern kingdom

(2) Hosea and Gomer (Hos. 1:2-9)

Hosea 1:2-9 introduces his exceptional marriage in Israelite society and his children. We can see here that YHWH controls his marriage and the naming of his children.YHWH uses his marriage and his family as a prophetic symbol previewing the coming judgment against the nation and the following fate of Israel.

> 2 When YHWH first spoke through Hosea, YHWH said to Hosea, "Go, take to yourself a wife of harlotry, and have children of harlotry; for the land commits flagrant harlotry, forsaking YHWH."
> 3 So he went and took Gomer the daughter of Diblaim, and she conceived and bore him a son.
> 4 And YHWH said to him, "Name him *Jezreel*; for yet a little while, and I will punish the house of Jehu for the bloodshed of Jezreel, and I will put an end to the kingdom of the house of Israel.
> 5 "And it will come about on that day, that I will break the bow of Israel in the valley of Jezreel."
> 6 Then she conceived again and gave birth to a daughter. And YHWH said to him, "Name her *Lo-ruhamah*, for I will no longer have compassion on the house of Israel, that I should ever forgive them.
> 7 "But I will have compassion on the house of Judah and deliver them by YHWH their God, and will not deliver them by bow, sword, battle, horses, or horsemen."
> 8 When she had weaned *Lo-ruhamah*, she conceived and gave birth to a son.
> 9 And YHWH said, "Name him *Lo-ammi*, for you are not my people and I am not your God."

Hos. 1:2-9 contains four commands of YHWH to do something, and *ki* (כִּי) clauses explain the reasons for them. YHWH commanded Hosea to take Gomer, a harlot, as his wife (2), and name their three children Jezreel (4),

The Marriage Texts

Lo-ruhamah (6), and Lo-ammi (9). This action and the names symbolize the future judgment of YHWH against Israel's apostasy. Thus, in this context YHWH gives warnings to his people through the symbolic act of the prophet Hosea. The same example can be seen in the names of *Shearjashub* (Isa. 7:3) and *Mahershalal-hash-baz* (Isa. 8:3), the children of Isaiah.

In verse 2, YHWH commanded Hosea, "Go, take to yourself a wife of harlotry, and have children of harlotry." The reason for this unusual marriage is that "the land commits flagrant harlotry, forsaking YHWH." Here, "Go, take to yourself a wife" is a typical phrase for describing marriage. "Go"(לך) usually describes a man's going to his bride's house to bring her to his house (Ex. 2:1). The Hebrew word *lāqaḥ* (לקח), rendered as "to take," is the most common marriage term. It denotes the idea of marriage as well as adoption.[3] When a man takes a woman, it represents marriage. However, it refers to adoption when a man takes a child or a man. The verb *lāqaḥ* (לקח) takes two objectives here. One is "a wife of harlotry" (אשת זנונים) and the other is "children of harlotry" (ילדי זנונים). Thus YHWH commands Hosea to take a wife of harlotry and adopt children of harlotry.[4] This would be a mockery in

---

3. Sohn, 11-16; 64-65. F. C. Fensham, "The Marriage Metaphor in Hosea for the Covenant Relationship between the Lord and his People," *JNSL* 12 (1984): 72. Seebass, *TWAT*, IV, 591-92. H. L. Ginsberg in M. Haran (ed), *Yehezjelkaufman Jubilee Volume* (Jerusalem: Magnes Press, 1960), 50. F. I. Andersen-D. N. Freedman, 156-57.

4. Certain commentators assert that "a wife of harlotry" does not refer to adulterous acts, rather it represents a woman's tendency to be adulterous or unfaithful to her husband. If this is correct, Gomer was a woman of virtue before her marriage, but she became unfaithful after the birth of her children; furthermore, the "children of harlotry" in verse 2 would refer to Hosea's three children from Gomer in verses 3-9. In this case it would be improper to call Gomer "a woman of harlotry" only because of her tendency without actual involvement in harlotry. And it would be more inappropriate to call the children the "children of harlotry" because of their mother's unfaithfulness, since they were born to a legally married couple. Cf. P. A. Kruger, "The Relationship between Yahweh and Israel as expressed by certain metaphors and similes in the book of Hosea."(D. Litt. dissertation, University of Stellenbosh, 1983), 13. F. I. Andersen-D. N. Freedman, 157 ff. an argument against it. C. Van Leeuwen, *Hosea* (POT; Nijkerk: G.F. Callenbach, 1984), 31.

Certain scholars assert that the Hebrew term should be אשה זונה instead of אשת זנונים as in the case of Josh. 2:1 and Judg. 11:1, if it does not refer to her tendency to be unfaithful rather than her adulterous acts. Moreover, they say that Gomer is not to be treated as a promiscuous woman since Hos. 1-3 does not concretely mention it. From this analogy, they try to interpret אשת זנונים figuratively. According to them, Israel committed spiritual harlotry,

the world and become a taunt to all. Everyone would regard Hosea as a mad man if the truth were known regarding this marriage. Therefore, why did YHWH give this severe command to his servant? It was because the land forsook YHWH and committed adultery. YHWH wanted to convince his people of their sins of apostasy by comparing it to Hosea's tragic marriage. Therefore, the book of Hosea portrays YHWH and Israel as a couple. Though the Israelites will laugh at Hosea's marriage to Gomer, a harlot with children of harlotry, YHWH's intent for this comparison is to teach them that Gomer symbolizes Israel herself.

Hosea took Gomer, a harlot, as his wife according to the command of YHWH. He gave birth to a son through Gomer and named him Jezreel (יזרעאל) as YHWH had commanded. The reason for this name is his recompense to the house of Jehu for the bloodshed of Jezreel and the coming fall of Israel. Thus, the name "Jezreel" will prefigure YHWH's future blood vengeance against the house of Jehu and the fall of the nation. The meaning of Jezreel is not as easy to define. This word is composed of $zāra^c$ (זרע, to sow, to plant) and $^{\circ}el$ (אל, God), and its meaning is "God planted," or "God sows." The name Jezreel in 1:11 or 2: 22-23 is used symbolically. However, it simply refers to the location and events that took place here. At Jezreel, Jehu eliminated the dynasty of Omri (2 Kgs 9:24-26) and massacred the family of Ahab, all his great men, his acquaintances, and his priests (2 Kgs 10:11). Jezreel was the valley of bloodshed. A great deal of innocent blood was shed there. Accordingly YHWH plans to repay the bloodshed of Jezreel to the house of Jehu and break the bow of Israel in the valley. "The bow of Israel" seems to refer to the military forces of Israel and "the breaking of the

---

since Israel worshipped the gentile gods and followed the pagan practices. Thus, Gomer is the one of the people of the days who was involved in religious apostasy, i.e., spiritual harlotry, not one who actually played the harlot.

However, אשת זונים is a characteristic genetive (GKC #128p -v) used attributively. It describes the woman whom Hosea was to marry. She was a woman of harlotry. זונים always describes the adulterous behavior of the woman beside Hosea. Thomas McComskey, *Hosea, An Exegetical & Expository Commentary: The Minor Prophets*, ed. Thomas Edward McComskey (Grand Rapids: Baker, 1992), 10-17. Therefore, if we understand אשת זונים as an abstract noun and it refers to the tendency of a woman, or it refers to Israel's apostasy as a metaphorical interpretation, it would diminish the role of the prophets and nullify the significance of the symbolic act and life of the prophet in denouncing the sins of Israel in his time.

bow of Israel" means the fall of Israel as indicated in verse 4. These phrases and images of breaking the bow can be found in the typical curse formula in ancient Near Eastern treaty texts.[5] *Jezreel*, the son of Hosea, thus, would be a member of the prophetic family foretelling the fall of Israel by his name.

Gomer again conceived and gave birth to a daughter (6). YHWH said to him to name her *Lo-ruhamah* and explained the reason for this as follows: "for I will no longer have compassion on the house of Israel, that I should ever forgive them. But I will have compassion on the house of Judah and deliver them by YHWH their God, and will not deliver them by bow, sword, battle, horses, or horsemen" (6-7). *Lo-ruhamah* is the composite word of *lo* (לא, not), the Hebrew negative and the verb, *rāḥam* (לחמ, to sympathize). YHWH is going to withdraw his love from his people. Israel will no longer be favored by YHWH. McComiskey observed the following structure in verses 6-7 and compared the fate of Judah and Israel.[6]

    a. I will no longer show love to the house of Israel.
        b. I will not forgive them (לא אשא להם).
    a'. I will have compassion on the house of Judah.
        b'. I will deliver them (הושעתים).

Here a-a' and b-b' constitute an antithetic parallelism. "No longer show love" and "have compassion on," and "not forgive them" and "deliver" are pairs of contrasting phrases. Whereas YHWH will not save the house of Israel, he will deliver the house of Judah. The deliverance of Judah is emphasized.

After Gomer had weaned *Lo-ruhamah*, she conceived and gave birth to a son. YHWH commanded that he be named *Lo-ammi*, because they will not be his people and he will not be their God. *Lo-ammi* is a composite word of *lō* (לא) and *ʿammî* (עמי, my people), which means "not my people." Thus, the name of the third child carries the meaning of a proclamation denouncing Israel as his people. "You are not my people and I am not your God" is a typical rejection formula.[7] This formula obviously borrowed from the

---

5. D. J. Wiseman, *The Vassal-Treaties of Esarhadon* (London: 1958), 63-64. F. C. Fensham, *The Covenant Idea in the Book of Hosea* (OTWSA, 1964-65), 44.

6. Thomas McComiskey, *Hosea* (An Exegetical & Expository Commentary: The Minor Prophets, ed. Thomas E. McComiskey. Grand Rapids: Baker, 1992), 25.

divorce formula, "I am not your husband and you are not my wife." This is also the negative form of the marriage formula, "I am your husband and you are my wife." Accordingly on the basis of this marriage relationship, YHWH is going to divorce his people because of their unfaithfulness, and he commanded that the son be named *Lo-ammi*, which is borrowed from the formula of divorce. These three names of Hosea's children show that a series of historical developments, the nullification of the Sinai covenant and the following curses and judgement toward Israel, are represented by the names *Jezreel* and *Lo-ruhamah* and YHWH's later rejection of Judah by the name *Lo-ammi*.

(3) YHWH and Israel (Hos. 1:10-2:23)

Hos. 1:1-9 depicts Hosea and his family as a sign and symbol of his times, carrying the message of the forthcoming judgment against Israel, the spouse of YHWH. However, Hos. 1:10-2:23 is the prophecy of YHWH's punishment for Israel's adultery and the following restoration of his people. Hos. 1:10-2:1 and 2:21-23 mention the glory of Jezreel, the land of bloodshed (11, 23), and the phrase "You are my people"(10; 2:1, 23) is used in the context of restoration. Israel's adultery (2:2-7), YHWH's punishment (8-13), and Israel's restoration (14-20) are the main subjects in this context. The following is the structure of 1:10-2:23.

    a. You are my people (1:10-2:1)
       b. Israel leaves YHWH and follows her lover (2:2-7)
          c. YHWH punishes Israel (2:8-13)
       b'. YHWH calls Israel to return (2:14-20)
    a'. You are my people (2:21-23)

This section begins with YHWH's promise of Israel's restoration and ends with Israel's restoration (a-a'). The paragraph a-a' seems to constitute an

---

7. *BHS* proposes to replace אהיה לכם with אלהיכם. However, it would be more fitting to insert אלהים between אהיה and לכם in order to correspond with the marriage formula. The phrase, thus, will be כי אתם לא עמי ואנכי לא־אהיה אלהים לכם (for you will not be my people and I will not be your God).

The Marriage Texts

inclusion. In b-c-b', c is the center of the antithetic parallelism of b-b'. Therefore, YHWH's message of restoration is the apex of this section.

a. You are my people (Hos. 1:10-2:1; 2:21-23)

10 [2:1]   Yet the number of the sons of Israel
Will be like the sand of the sea
Which can not be measured or numbered;
And it will come about that, in the place
Where it is said to them,
"You are not my people,"
It will be said to them,
"You are the sons of the living God."

11 [2:2]   And the sons of Judah and the sons of
Israel will be gathered together,
And they will appoint for themselves one leader,
And they will go up from the land,
For great will be the day of Jezreel.

2:1[2:3]   Say to your brothers, "Ammi,"
And to your sister, "Ruhamah."

Whereas Hos.1:2-9 describes YHWH's rejection of Israel because of her harlotry (symbolized in Hosea's marriage and the names of his children), 1:10-2:2 describes his restoration of Israel. Even though YHWH denounces Israel saying "You are not my people and I will not be your God"(1:9), Israel will be multiplied like the sand of the sea which cannot be measured or numbered. Where it is said to them, "You are not my people," it will be said to them, "You are the sons of the living God"(10). The promise of descendents to Abraham (Gen. 22:17) is again given to them. Here, Israel is not referred to as the "children of God," not as the spouse of YHWH or as his people. Someday the sons of Judah and Israel will be gathered together and they will appoint one leader for themselves and come up from the land of Jezreel because it is Jezreel which God has planted. The term "come up" (עלה) expresses the budding of a plant or vegetables coming up from the land, and it refers to the restoration of Israel. When they come up, YHWH will say to them, "*Ammi* to your brothers, and *Ruhamah* to your sisters"(2:1). YHWH proposes reconciliation to the people once called *Lo-ammi* and *Lo-*

ruhamah. The "one leader" seems to refer to YHWH himself, not to any human leader. He will unite Judah and Israel together and will bring them back from captivity. Once the day of Jezreel was the day of bloodshed, but it will be changed to the day of glory. However, the day will be so glorious that *Lo-ruhammah* is called *ruhammah* and *Lo-ammi* is called *ami*. This obviously refers to YHWH's restoration of the rejected Israel as well as the salvation of the gentiles.

b. Israel leaves YHWH and follows her lover (Hos. 2:2-7)

Hosea compares Israel to an adulterous wife who has followed her lover leaving her husband behind.

2[4]		Contend with your mother, contend
		For she is not my wife, and I am not her husband;
		And let her put away her harlotry from her face,
		And her adultery from between her breasts.
3[5]		Lest I strip her naked
		And expose her as on the day when she was born,
		I will also make her like a wilderness,
		Make her like desert land,
		And slay her with thirst.
4[6]		Also, I will have no compassion on her children,
		Because they are children of harlotry.
5[7]		For their mother has played the harlot;
		She who conceived them has acted shamefully.
		For she said, "I will go after my lovers,
		Who gave me my bread and my water,
		My wool and my flax, my oil and my drink."
6[8]		Therefore, behold, I will hedge up her way with thorns,
		And I will build a wall against her so that she cannot find her paths.
7[9]		And she will pursue her lovers, but she will not overtake them;
		And she will seek them, but will not find them.
		Then she will say, "I will go back to my first husband,
		For it was better for me then than now!"

This is basically the husband's accusation of his wife's adultery. The term *rib* (ריב), translated as "contend," is a legal term used in the court. It also carries the meaning of "to plead" (1Sam. 25:39; Ps. 35:1; 119: 154; Isa. 3:13; Lam. 3:58), or "to contend"(Gen. 26:22; Job 9:3). However, "to persuade" fits this situation more accurately because the demand is the practical act of removing the harlotry.[8] Both the mother and children refer to Israel. More precisely, the mother refers to Israel in the collective sense of the word and the children refer to the individual Israel. We need to take notice of the phrase, "I am not your husband and you are not my wife" in YHWH's lawsuit against Israel. This presupposes a marriage relationship between YHWH and Israel. This phrase completely conforms to 1:9, "You are not my people and I am not your God" in its form and meaning. This phrase does not specify when YHWH and Israel entered into the marriage relationship. The relationship, perhaps, was widely recognized among the people of Israel at that time. Unfortunately this relationship was broken. YHWH is persuading his people to remove their harlotry through their children before he imposes punishment on them. Usually harlots painted their faces (Jer. 4:30; Ezek. 23:40) and used a bundle of myrrh between their breasts (SS. 1:13) as an aprodisiac.[9]

In verse 2 (Heb. 5), the Hebrew conjunction *pen* (פן), which is translated as "lest," governs the following 5 clauses: "I strip her," "expose her," "make her like a wilderness," "make her like a desert land," and "slay her with thirst." These phrases describe the status of Israel before her election by YHWH (6-7). If Israel, designated here as a mother, would not remove the marks of a prostitute, YHWH will reject her and she will eventually be removed from existence. She will return to the status she had before her marriage with YHWH. YHWH had to accuse her and impose on her capital punishment as prescribed in the Law of Moses for those who commit adultery. YHWH punishes not only the adulterous wife but also her children (4). He will not have compassion on her children because they are the children of harlotry. The people of Israel worshiped and served the gentile gods. Their descendants also became worshipers of Baal after the manner of

---

8. Mckomskey, 32. H. B. Huffmon, "The Covenant Lawsuit in the Prophets," *JBL* 78 (1959): 295-95. D. J. McCarthy, *Old Testament Covenant: A Survey of Current Opinion* (Atlanta: John Knox, 1972), 38-40. J. Linberg, "The Root, *RIB* and Prophetic Lawsuit Speeches," *JBL* 88(1969): 291-304.

9. Francis I. Anderson and David N. Freedman, *Hosea*, 224.

their ancestors. YHWH calls these descendants "children of harlotry" and proclaims *Lo-ruhamah* (I will no longer have compassion on the house of Israel) and *Lo-ammi* (You are not my people).

In verses 5-7 (Heb. 7-9) the details of the mother's harlotry are provided. A husband had to provide his wife with her domicile, food, and clothes and the wife should be completely dependent on her husband. However, the wife referred to here followed her lover because he seduced her by offering her bread, water, wool, flax, oil and drink. YHWH will not tolerate her betrayal. He will hedge up her way with thorns. She cannot find him and overtake him. At last she will come back to her first husband saying "For it was better for me then than now." Hosea is here describing the follies of Israel who has followed the gentile gods with the expectation of full provision for the daily supplies but returned empty handed. YHWH is strong enough to block her way from following her lover. He will not let her be seduced and leave him.

Thus, verses 2-7 describe the adulterous wife who deserts her family and follows her lover. This is an obvious metaphor comparing the YHWH-Israel relationship to that of Hosea and his adulterous wife. YHWH and Israel here are described as a husband and wife.

c. *YHWH punishes Israel (Hos. 2:8-13)*

When YHWH blocked Israel's way from following her lover, her adulterous behavior was revealed and a corresponding punishment was imposed. Verses 8-13 are pivotal in the chiastic structure of 1:10-2:23.

8 [10]	"For she does not know that it was I who gave her the grain, the new wine, and the oil, and lavished on her silver and gold, which they used for Baal.
9 [11]	Therefore, I will take back my grain at harvest time and my new wine in its season. I will also take away my wool and my flax given to cover her nakedness.
10 [12]	And then I will uncover her lewdness in the sight of her lovers, and no one will rescue her out of my hand.
11 [13]	I will also put an end to all her gaiety, her feasts, her new moons, her sabbaths, and all her festal assemblies.

The Marriage Texts

12[13]   And I will destroy her vines and fig trees, of which she said, 'These are my wages which my lovers have given me.' And I will make them a forest, and the beasts of the field will devour them.

13[14]   And I will punish her for the days of the Baals when she used to offer sacrifices to them and adorn herself with her earrings and jewelry, and follow her lovers, so that she forgot me," declares YHWH.

Baal is first mentioned here as a lover of Israel (10, 15). YHWH, as the faithful husband, gave Israel all the necessities for living such as food, clothes, gold and silver decorations, etc. However, Israel did not know that these were given by YHWH. She even offered and sacrificed them to Baal, her lover. YHWH, in revenge, was going to take back the food and clothes he had given to her and strip her of her clothing, revealing her lewdness in the sight of her lovers. No one will be able to rescue her out of his strong hand. YHWH's retribution against the betrayer is highlighted by his exposing her nakedness. He will also reveal the helplessness and weakness of her lover before the Almighty. Furthermore, he will abolish all her feasts and festivals such as those for the new moons and sabbath, etc. He will also destroy the vines and fig trees, and the beasts of the field will devour them. The land will be changed to a forest and the wild animals will make their nests there. YHWH will punish his people for the days they served Baal. In the long run, Israel will be fallen because of their apostasy. It is here to be noted that YHWH is described as the husband of Israel. Israel is his wife who has followed her lover and was later deserted by her husband as well as her lover with an eventual divorce from her husband.

d. YHWH calls Israel to return (Hos. 2:14-20)

Verses 14-20 (Heb 16-22) describe YHWH's restoration of Israel after his punishment. He goes to her and takes her as his wife again. This paragraph is a metaphor of the remarriage between YHWH and Israel.

14[16]   'Therefore, behold, I will allure her, bring her into the wilderness, and speak kindly to her.

15[17]   Then I will give her her vineyards from there, and the valley of Achor as a door of hope. And she will sing there as in the days of her youth, as in the day when she came up from the land of Egypt.

16[18] And it will come about in that day," declares YHWH, "That you will call me *Ishi* and will no longer call me *Baali*.
17[19] For I will remove the names of the Baals from her mouth, so that they will be mentioned by their names no more.
18[20] In that day I will also make a covenant for them with the beasts of the field, the birds of the sky, and the creeping things of the ground. And I will abolish the bow, the sword, and war from the land, and will make them lie down in safety.
19[21] And I will betroth you to me forever; yes, I will betroth you to me in righteousness and in justice, in lovingkindness and in compassion,
20[22] And I will betroth you to me in faithfulness. Then you will know YHWH."

The first step for YHWH to restore Israel was to allure her to come back to him. The Hebrew verb *paṭā* (פתה) can be rendered as "to woo," "to speak tenderly," "to allure." YHWH will allure and comfort her with a tender voice. He will bring her to the wilderness and give her a vineyard there and make the valley of Achor as a door of hope. The day of restoration will, thus, be like that of the exodus. The meaning of bringing her into the wilderness is seen as an engagement as in Jer. 2:2.

The vineyard was a gift from YHWH to Israel at the time of the exodus. However, Israel forgot this and believed it was given to her by Baal, her lover, as a reward for her love. YHWH thus devastated the vineyard. He made it the field of animals and the nests of wild beasts (12). But now YHWH changes his mind and takes Israel again as his wife and gives it back to her. He returns the land and its abundant products to Israel as his gift. YHWH demonstrates and confirms that he is the sole provider for Israel, not Baal. The valley of Achor, meaning "the valley of trouble," was the place Achan was executed at the time of the conquest of Jericho. He violated the *ḥelem* (חרם, the things banned) and he took the spoils of gold and silver and a mantle. For the punishment of this, he became *ḥelem* (חרם, Josh. 6:18; 7:16-26). The valley was thus the place of betrayal against YHWH and the following judgment, execution and death. Nevertheless, the place of curses will be turned into a gate leading to hope. This is the promise of YHWH's full forgiveness and complete restoration of Israel. Obviously the day Israel is restored will be like the day of YHWH brought her out from Egypt.

The second step in YHWH's restoration of Israel was to eradicate all memories of her lover from Israel. The Hebrew nouns *ʾîš* (אישׁ) and *bāʾal* (בעל) are both rendered as "husband." *Bāʾal* (בעל) is a homonym with the name of Israel's lover, the Canaanite fertility gods. When the wives of Israel mentioned their husbands ("my husband"), this could be pronounced either as *ʾîšî* (אישׁי) or *bāʾalî* (בעלי). If a wife said *bāʾalî* (בעלי), it would not be easy to discern whether she called "My husband!" or "My god, Baal!" Therefore, YHWH commands Israel to use only the word *ʾîš* (אישׁ). In this way, YHWH is going to prohibit her from using the term *bāʾal* (בעל) and even from remembering the name of her lover. YHWH's effort to eradicate the memory of love and lover from Israel was the second step of restoration.

The third step for YHWH's restoration of Israel was to make a covenant with Israel. Marriage is a kind of covenant carrying legal force. In ancient Near Eastern society a marriage contract was drawn up. Likewise, YHWH also makes a covenant as he enters again into a marriage relationship with Israel. YHWH promises to provide Israel with a safe and comfortable house. In the ancient world the most threatening elements for the inhabitants of the land might have been the wild beasts or war between the tribes. In order to protect his people from those dangers, YHWH made a covenant with the beasts of the field, the birds of the sky, and the creeping things of the ground. He will also abolish all the instruments of war such as the bow, the sword and even war itself from the land (18). Then YHWH will be betrothed to Israel with all types of virtues such as righteousness, justice, lovingkindness, and compassion. All these virtues are ties binding the covenant partners together.[10] Therefore, the reunion is much stronger than the original union. When YHWH is betrothed to Israel with those virtues, Israel will know him. Here it is to be noted that the Hebrew verb *yādaʿ* (ידע) is used. It implies various aspects of the renewed relationship between YHWH and Israel since the term is used for describing the most intimate relations between husband and wife.

e. You are my people (Hos. 2:21-23)

10. F. I. Anderson (*Hosea*, 283) and H. W. Wolf propose that these five virtues are the bridal price that YHWH gave to his bride, Israel(*Hosea*, 52). However, this does not fit with the context of a covenant in 20-24.

YHWH, THE HUSBAND OF ISRAEL

Hos. 2:21-23 describes the restored relationship between YHWH and his people. This paragraph constitutes a symmetrical parallelism with 1:10-2:1. YHWH and Israel respond to each other: "You are my people," and "you are my God." The restoration of the Jezreel valley is also mentioned.

> 21[23] "In that day I will respond," declares YHWH "I will respond to the skies, and they will respond to the earth;
> 22[24] and the earth will respond to the grain, the new wine and oil, and they will respond to Jezreel.
> 23[25] I will plant her for myself in the land; I will show my love to the one I called 'Not my loved one.' I will say to those called 'Not my people,' 'You are my people'; and they will say, 'You are my God.'"

One of the main events in the course of YHWH's restoration of his wife, Israel, is the restoration of nature. When their relationship is reestablished, YHWH will respond to the skies, and they will respond to the earth, and the earth will respond to the grain, the new wine and oil, and they will respond to Jezreel. The Hebrew verb ʿānā (ענה) means "to answer," "to respond." It is used when YHWH takes action or is involved in events to provide the needs of people or things (Ps. 20:1; Isa. 41:17; 49:8; Hos. 14:9). The skies, the earth, the grain and wine, and Jezreel establish a chain relationship and each respond to the other successively. The initiator of this chain relationship is YHWH. He initiates the prime movement of the chain responses. The restoration of the YHWH-Israel relationship brings order to nature and its productive activity.

The confirmation of the covenant is the last step for the restoration. YHWH will say to those who were not his people, "You are my people!" As a response they will say, "You are my God!" Obviously these are borrowed from the marriage formula: "You are my husband, you are my wife." This also parallels the negative form of the divorce formula: "You are not my wife, you are not my husband." YHWH's restoration of Israel will be concluded by the confirmation of the covenant as in marriage.

(4) YHWH and Hosea (Hos. 3:1-5)

The Marriage Texts

The third chapter of Hosea describes the restored relationship between Hosea and his wife on the basis of YHWH-Israel's restored relationship.

1. Then YHWH said to me, "Go again, love a woman who is loved by her husband, yet an adulteress, even as YHWH loves the sons of Israel, though they turn to other gods and love raisin cakes."
2. So I bought her for myself for fifteen shekels of silver and a homer and a half of barley.
3. Then I said to her, "You shall stay with me for many days. You shall not play the harlot, nor shall you have a man; so I will also be toward you."
4. For the sons of Israel will remain for many days without king or prince, without sacrifice or sacred pillar, and without ephod or household idols.
5. Afterward the sons of Israel will return and seek YHWH their God and David their king; and they will come trembling to YHWH and to his goodness in the last days.

Hosea was commanded to love his wife again after she had followed her lover, and he was to buy her back by paying for her in silver and barley. The reason for this command was that YHWH loved the sons of Israel even though they turned to other gods and loved raisin cakes (1). As YHWH accepted Israel as his people, those who were no longer his people because they had played the harlot, Hosea also was to accept his adulterous wife as his spouse. According to the law of Moses, the reunion of a divorced couple was abominable in the eyes of YHWH and was thus prohibited. However, YHWH himself practiced love that went beyond the law and commanded Hosea to show the same love toward his wife. Therefore, he bought her for fifteen shekels of silver and a homer and a half of barley. Moreover, he implored her not to leave him for many days, not to play the harlot, and not to have another man. In the same way, Israel will be returned to YHWH after many days of her apostasy. The term "afterward" (אחר) seems to refer to the eschatological age (Isa. 2:2; Jer. 49:39; Ezek. 38:8,16; Dan. 10:14; Mic. 4:1). Accordingly this restoration points to the messianic age that has long been promised by YHWH. With this in mind, Hos. 3 can be analyzed as follows:

a. YHWH still loves his apostate Israel (1a)
b. Hosea loves his adulterous wife again (1b-2)
c. The adulterous wife returns to Hosea (3)
d. Israel returns to YHWH (4)

YHWH, THE HUSBAND OF ISRAEL

Verses 1-2 describe YHWH and Hosea, both of whom love their apostate wives. Verses 3-4 show Israel and the adulterous wife who have been moved by their spouse's forgiveness and returned to their husband.

As has been observed, Hosea 1-3 has an organic unity in its content. In Hos. 1:2-9, YHWH takes the initiative in the marriage of Hosea and Gomer and the naming of their children which implied the forthcoming fate of Israel. Hos. 1:10-2:23 describes Gomer's unfaithfulness to her husband as well as Israel's apostasy against YHWH. However, the main emphasis lies not in Israel's rebellion but in YHWH's restoration of Israel. Hos. 3:1-5 is also about YHWH's restoration of Hosea's marriage. Thus we can see that the message of Hos. 1-3 does not point to the punishment of the adulterous Gomer and apostate Israel, but to YHWH's salvation and restoration of the fallen family and nation because of their sins.

Again it is evident here that YHWH's election, covenant, rejection and restoration of Israel are compared to Hosea's marriage, divorce, and remarriage with Gomer. The relationship of YHWH with Israel is intimate, personal and covenantal, just as a marriage relationship is, carrying full legal force. Since a covenant entails sanction, it always claims proper punishment on the unfaithful partner. Accordingly, both kingdoms of the South and the North will be destroyed as YHWH said. YHWH prohibits the reunion of a divorced couple in the Law. However, contradictorily, he accepts Israel, his adulterous wife, whom he wants to love and save. YHWH commands Hosea to take his wife again. The book of Hosea is a reflection of the relationship between YHWH and Israel, both of whom are bound by a covenant. The description of this relationship obviously borrows from the illustration of human marriage.

2. THE BOOK OF JEREMIAH

Jeremiah was the prophets whose concern was mainly about the relationship between YHWH and Israel, describing it in terms of the metaphor of marriage or adoption. In particular, his keen interest in the covenant relationship is observed throughout his book. Since he perceived that the fall of the northern kingdom was brought on by Israel's unfaithfulness to the covenant

The Marriage Texts

with YHWH, Jeremiah exhorted the southern kingdom not to follow in the steps of the northerners and to be faithful to the covenant. He, thus, renewed the covenant with YHWH, celebrated the passover, and proclaimed the sabbatical year so that they might have remission of debts or set free their male and female servants (Jer. 34:8-11). Jeremiah understood the nature of the relationship between YHWH and Israel in terms of a covenant as a marriage realationship was understood as a kind of covenant in the ancient Near Eastern world.

(1) Jeremiah 2:1-37

Jeremiah 2 is not easy to establish as a text which uses the marriage metaphor because it not only vividly describes Israel's rebellion against YHWH, but it also employs complex images and metaphors such as husband and wife (2, 23-25, 31-33), father and son (27, 29), and farmer and vineyard (3, 21). However, the central point of Jer. 2 is YHWH's rebuke against Israel's apostasy in which she has forsaken her covenant with him and worshiped Baal. Her behavior is described in terms of the metaphor of marriage and divorce.

In verse 2, YHWH said, "I remember concerning you the devotion of your youth, the love of your betrothals, your following after me in the wilderness." As observed earlier, "the love of marriage" is more proper than "the love of betrothals."[11] Jeremiah portrays the journey of YHWH leading Israel through the wilderness to Canaan after the exodus as a bridegroom who brings his bride to his home from her father's house after engagement. In verses 23-25 he compares Israel to a swift young camel or a wild donkey that is in her passion and in the time of her heat. Israel was already the wife of YHWH and was to be faithful to him. But she went to her lover, the one her husband hated, in order to satisfy her sexual desires. In verses 31-33 Jeremiah describes YHWH's regret concerning the unfaithfulness of Israel in forgetting him who had given various gifts to her. This can be seen in comparison to the popular idea of a bride, who would not usually forget her groom's gift. YHWH is here portrayed as the faithful husband. However, his bride is not

11. Cf. Chapter II, 1 (6).

faithful to him. This theme is further dealt with in the third chapter of Jeremiah.

(2) Jeremiah 3:1-18

The third chapter of Jeremiah describes YHWH's accusation of apostasy against Judah and Israel and his earnest plea for them to return to him in order that he might heal them. Jeremiah borrowed the imagery of a husband-wife and father-son and compared Israel's apostasy to the adultery of a wife or to a son who has left his father. He even combined these two images and allegorized them. Thus, we find complex metaphors in Jer. 3. A foreknowledge of the historical background is a prerequisite for a proper understanding of this text.

In verse 6, Jeremiah states that he received this word from YHWH during the reign of Josiah (640-609 B.C.). This was almost 80 years after the northern kingdom fell to Assyria and approximately 100 years after Hosea described the YHWH-Israel relationship in terms of a husband-wife metaphor. Josiah was responsible for the reformation of the religion of Judah. During the reigns of his predecessors, such as Ahaz and Manasseh, the gentile religions prevailed in Judah. In particular, the apostasy of Manasseh played a decisive role in the fall of the nation (2 Kgs. 21:10-15). The book of Kings describes the practice of Manasseh as follows:

1 Manasseh was twelve years old when he became king, and he reigned fifty-five years in Jerusalem; and his mother's name was Hephzibah.
2 And he did evil in the sight of YHWH, according to the abominations of the nations whom YHWH dispossessed before the sons of Israel.
3 For he rebuilt the high places which Hezekiah his father had destroyed; and he erected altars for Baal and made an Asherah, as Ahab king of Israel had done, and worshiped all the host of heaven and served them.
4 And he built altars in the house of YHWH, of which YHWH had said, "In Jerusalem I will put my name."
5 For he built altars for all the host of heaven in the two courts of the house of YHWH.
6 And he made his son pass through the fire, practiced witchcraft and used divination, and dealt with mediums and spiritists. He did much evil in the

sight of YHWH provoking him to anger.
7 Then he set the carved image of Asherah that he had made, in the house of which YHWH said to David and to his son Solomon, "In this house and in Jerusalem, which I have chosen from all the tribes of Israel, I will put my name forever.
8 "And I will not make the feet of Israel wander anymore from the land which I gave their fathers, if only they will observe to do according to all that I have commanded them, and according to all the law that my servant Moses commanded them."
9 But they did not listen, and Manasseh seduced them to do evil more than the nations whom YHWH destroyed before the sons of Israel. (2 Kgs 21:1-9)

Manasseh turned back the direction of religious reformation by rebuilding the high places which his father had destroyed and erecting altars for Baal and making an Asherah. He completely took the way of apostasy and provoked YHWH to anger. He even built altars for all the hosts of heaven in the two courts of the temple and had his son pass through the fire. He practiced witchcraft and used divination and dealt with mediums and spiritists. Thus YHWH proclaimed judgment on him through Nathan, his prophet. "Because Manasseh king of Judah has done these abominations, having done wickedly more than all the Amorites did who were before him, and has also made Judah sin with his idols; therefore, thus says YHWH, the God of Israel, Behold, I am bringing such calamity on Jerusalem and Judah, that whoever hears of it, both his ears shall tingle"(2 Kgs 21:11-12). What does it mean that Manasseh had done wickedly more than all the Amorites? YHWH cast the Amorites out of the land of Canaan because of their iniquities and settled the Israelites there instead (Gen. 15:16; 1Kgs. 25:26). Now the fate of Judah is evident if her wickedness is more than that of the Amorites. Judah will surely be destroyed.

The rebellious activities of Judah against YHWH were temporarily checked by Josiah, the successor of Amon, the son of Manasseh who was assassinated. Josiah's reformation was greatly indebted to the weakness of the Assyrian's military forces at the western fronts. He purged the land of all types of Assyrian rituals and gentile practices and cleansed the temple. In 622 BC, the book of the Law was found in the process of repairing the damage that had been done to the temple. Josiah assembled all his people and read all the words of God written in the book and made a covenant before YHWH "to walk after YHWH, and keep his commandments and his testimonies and his statues with all his heart and his soul, to carry out the words of this covenant that were written in this book"(2 Kgs 23:4). He commanded the people to celebrate the Passover as it was written in the Law. Furthermore, he proclaimed Jerusalem as a unique place of worship for YHWH and commanded that all other places of worship be demolished and destroyed (2 Kgs23:15, 19, 20).

If we take this historical background into account, it can be deduced that Jer. 3:1-10 was given at the beginning of Josiah's reign when the effects of Manasseh's apostasy were still alive in the minds of the people. The third chapter of Jeremiah is composed of two parts: a poetical section (1-5; 12-13; 19-25) and a prose section (6-11; 14-18). These two sections are arranged alternatively. In Jer. 3:1-10 the first half (1-5) is a poem, and the latter half (6-10) is in the form of prose.

1. God says, "If a husband divorces his wife, and she goes from him and belongs to another man, will he still return to her? Will not that land be completely polluted? But you are a harlot with man lovers; Yet you turn to me," declares YHWH.
2. "Lift up your eyes to the bare heights and see; Where have you not been violated? By the roads you have sat for them like an Arab in the desert, and you have polluted a land with your harlotry and with your wickedness.
3. "Therefore the showers have been withheld, and there has been no spring rain. Yet you had a harlot's forehead; you refused to be ashamed.
4. "Have you not just now called to me, 'My Father, Thou art the friend of my youth?
5. 'Will he be angry forever? Will he be indignant to the end?' Behold, you have spoken and have done evil things, and you have had your way."
6. Then YHWH said to me in the days of Josiah the king, 'Have you seen what faithless Israel did? She went up on every high hill and under every green tree, and she was a harlot there.
7. "And I thought, 'After she has done all these things, she will return to me'; but she did not return, and her treacherous sister Judah saw it.
8. "And I saw that for all the adulteries of faithless Israel, I had sent her away and given her a writ of divorce, yet her treacherous sister Judah did not fear; but she went and was a harlot also.
9. "And it came about because of the lightness of her harlotry, that she polluted the land and committed adultery with stones and trees.
10. "And yet in spite of all this her treacherous sister Judah did not return to me with all her heart, but rather in deception," declares YHWH.

The Marriage Texts

11 And YHWH said to me, "Faithless Israel has peoved herself more righteous than treacherous Judah.
12 "Go, and proclaim these words toward the north and say, 'return, faithless Israel,' declares YHWH; 'I will not look upon you in anger. For I am gracious,' declares YHWH; 'I will not be angry forever.
13 'Only acknowledge your iniquity, that you have transgressed against YHWH your God and have scattered your favors to the strangers under every green tree, and you have not obeyed my voice,' declares YHWH.
14. 'Return, O faithless sons,' declares YHWH; 'for I am a master to you, and I will take you one from a city and two from a family; and I will bring you to Zion.
15 Then I will give you shepherds after my own heart, who will feed you on knowledge and understanding.
16 "And it shall be in those days when you are multiplied and increased in the land," declares YHWH, "they shall say no more, 'The ark of the covenant of YHWH.' And it shall not come to mind, nor shall they remember it, nor shall they miss it, nor it be made again.
17 At that time they shall call Jerusalem 'The throne of YHWH,' and all the nations will gathered to it, for the name of YHWH in Jerusalem; nor shall they walk any more after the stubbornness of their evil heart.
18 In those days the house of Judah will walk with the house of Israel, and they will come together from the land of the north to the land that I gave your fathers as an inheritance.

The poetical section of this paragraph begins with the rhetorical question: Will the husband still return to his divorced wife who now belongs to another man? Of course, a negative answer is expected on the basis of Deut. 24:1-4. We do not know the exact reason for this practice. However, some scholars have proposed that a married couple still maintained a brother-sister relationship even after their divorce. Accordingly the remarriage of a divorced couple would result in incest within the circle of close kinsmen, and that is the reason why such a reunion is prohibited in the law. Others give the explanation that the purpose of this law was to protect the second marriage of the divorced woman. Whatever reasons there might be, the reunion of a divorced couple was prohibited at the time of Jeremiah. Since this is the case, YHWH asked again, will not that land be completely polluted? In the Old Testament, human beings and the land are closely interrelated. Nature has always been affected by the sins of man. This is because nature is under the headship of man in the covenantal structure of the created world before God. Because of Adam's sin, the earth had to produce thorns and thistles (Gen.

3:18). Evil and the sins of human beings brought a curse on the earth and the desolation of the land (Lev. 18:25, 28; 19:29; Deut. 24:4; Hos. 4:2,3; Amos 4:6-10). Besides this, the land carries a special meaning for the people of Israel. YHWH, as a groom, gave the land to Israel as a domicile for his bride. It was a holy land because YHWH himself dwelt there with his people. In the very place of his abode, Israel played the harlot. Therefore, YHWH contends with his people about their crooked relationship by showing the unacceptable practice of remarriage between divorced couples. Even though Israel played the harlot with many others, she wanted to come back to him without showing any regret in her mind. Thus YHWH said, "But you are a harlot with many lovers; yet you turn to me"(2). God forgives the sinner when he repents and confesses his sin with a contrite heart, showing his resolution to obey God's commandments faithfully. However, such genuine repentance was not found among the people of Israel. YHWH, thus, pointed to the bare heights and commanded them to see them. The bare heights are the small mountains without any grass or trees. In the Bible,the Hebrew word $š^ep\bar{a}yim$ (שׁפים) always refers to the top of a mountain where the sacrifices were offered to Baal(3:2, 21; 4:11; 7:29; 12:12; 14:6). It does not refer to the rocky hills or mountains without trees, rather to those heights made desolate because so many people have tread on them in order to offer sacrifices that trees were broken and glasses were smashed. YHWH commanded the people to lift up their eyes and see the barren heights and asked, "Where have you not been violated?"(2). YHWH had them look back at their rebellious footprints. Then he compares them to a woman waiting for passersby in order to play the harlot with them, like Arabian merchants in the desert sat and waited for customers by the roads. The people of Israel had polluted the entire land with their harlotry and their wickedness. In consequence, showers had been withheld and the spring rains had ceased. Baal, the god Israel had served, was believed to be a fertility god as well as a rain god that caused various grains and vegetables to grow. However, Baal could not give them rain. Nevertheless, the people of Israel refused to be ashamed of their behavior. They carried the mark of a harlot on their foreheads.

Afterwards Israel remembered YHWH and thought of returning to him and said, "My father, you are the friend of my youth? Will he be angry forever? Will he be indignant to the end?" They cried for rain and reminded YHWH of his mercy at the time of the exodus and their settlement in Canaan

The Marriage Texts

when he fed and protected them as a father would his children. However, they would not return completely and come to YHWH. Rather they continued their evil behavior and clung to their father's affection, trusting that he would never punish his son. YHWH regards Israel as a wife who has forsaken her husband and followed her lover, but Israel regards herself as a child who is loved but who has no sense of the seriousness of her actions. Israel had a double mind. On the one hand she served Baal who could not give her rain, and on the other hand she longed for YHWH. However, she was reluctant to return to him. Israel was still syncretistic, and YHWH called her a harlot.

Verses 6-10 describe the apostasy of Judah and Israel more vividly and practically. YHWH opens his mouth in order to explain the evils of Israel by asking Jeremiah, "Have you seen what faithless Israel did?" Judah and Israel are here portrayed as sisters as well as being the wives of YHWH. Israel "went up on every high hill and under every green tree and she was a harlot there"(6). YHWH saw this and thought that they would come back to him after they finished all those things. YHWH, as a husband, waits for and expects his adulterous wife's return. However, Israel did not come back. The Hebrew word $m^e\check{s}\underline{b}\bar{a}$ (משבה), rendered as "faithless," is a derivative of $\check{s}\hat{u}\underline{b}$ (שוב), meaning "return to," or "return from." Thus, the designation of $m^e\check{s}u\underline{b}\bar{a}$ $yi\acute{s}ra^{\jmath}\bar{e}l$ (משבה ישראל), refers to Israel who has turned to other gods and left YHWH. He expected $m^e\check{s}u\underline{b}\bar{a}$ $yi\acute{s}ra^{\jmath}\bar{e}l$ (משבה ישראל) to return (שוב) to him. But they did not return ($l\bar{o}^{\jmath}$ $\check{s}\bar{a}\underline{b}\bar{a}$, לא שבה).[12] Accordingly YHWH said, "for all the adulteries of faithless Israel, I had sent her away and given her a writ of divorce" (8).

Verses 3:11-18 describe YHWH's invitation of Israel to repentence and the promise of restoration. The phrases, "Return, faithless Israel"(12), "Only acknowledge your iniquity"(13), "Return, O faithless sons"(14), etc. directly describe YHWH's call for repentance. YHWH's invitation to repentance is based on the previous relationship established between them, a father-son and husband-wife relationship. YHWH calls Israel "faithless sons." Thus he portrays himself as a father who is waiting for his sons to return to him. And in verse 14, YHWH identifies himself as a "master." However, the Hebrew verb $ba^calt\hat{\imath}$ (בעלתי) means "to marry." The phrase, $k\hat{\imath}$ $^{\jmath}\bar{a}\underline{n}ok\hat{\imath}$ $b\bar{a}^calt\hat{\imath}$ $\underline{b}a\underline{k}em$

---

12. Peter C. Craigie, etc. *Jeremiah 1-25.* 26, 55.

YHWH, THE HUSBAND OF ISRAEL

(כי אנכי בעלתי בכם, for I married to you) in verse 14 is a typical marriage formula used in describing the marriage status. Israel rebelled against YHWH their God and scattered their favors to the strangers under the every green trees. They have not obeyed his voice. But YHWH says that he is gracious and will not look upon them in anger (12). Even he says he will not be angry forever. Thus he asks them only to acknowledge their iniquity and come back to him. And he promises that he will give them shepherds after his own heart, who will feed them on knwoledge and understanding. At that time Jerusalem will be called to be "The Throne of YHWH" and all the nations will be gathered to it. And Judah and Israel will also come togrther from the north to the land of their inheritance.

It is noteworthy here that YHWH condemns Israel for committing adultery because she left him and served other gods and did not return to him. Further he said to send her away and gave her a writ of divorce. This condemnation and the following prescription of a penalty presupposes a marriage relation between him and Israel. In Jer. 2:2 YHWH said, "I remember concerning you the devotion of your youth, the love of your betrothals, your following after me in the wilderness through a land not sown." YHWH portrays Israel's wandering in the wilderness after the exodus as a bridegroom bringing his bride to his house and the bride following after her groom toward her new domicile. However, this kind of loving relationship has already been broken because of her treacherous behavior. YHWH now takes the legal action of divorce against his adulterous wife as prescribed in Deut. 24:1-3. If YHWH divorced and sent Israel away, what event does he refer this to in the history of Israel?

During the period of Josiah's reign, the northern kingdom had already fallen and was no longer in existence (722 BC, 2 Kgs 17:1-18). The king of Assyria invaded the whole land and captured Samaria and carried Israel away into exile to Assyria. He settled them in Halah and Habor, on the river of Gozan, and in the cities of the Medes. In their place, he brought men from Babylon, Cuthah, Avva, Hamath, and Sepharvaim and settled them in the cities of Samaria (2 Kgs. 17:23-24). When YHWH took Israel for his people, he delivered them from Egypt and made the covenant which is portrayed as a wedding. Furthermore, he settled them in the promised land. YHWH gave Israel the land where they settled as a groom prepares a dwelling place for his bride. Israel, however, betrayed YHWH and left him and did not return. Now

The Marriage Texts

YHWH had to take action against her apostasy. He drove Israel out of the land of Canaan that he had given her on the day of marriage and sent her away to an unknown place with a writ of divorce in her hands. Thus YHWH describes his relationship with Israel in terms of the metaphor of marriage and divorce.

What was the response of Judah to the fate of her sister Israel? YHWH said, "Yet her treacherous sister Judah did not fear, but she went and was a harlot also"(Jer. 3:8). Judah, the sister of Israel, followed in her sister's wake and committed adultery with stones and trees (9). The leaders of Judah, the kings, princes, priests and prophets say to the tree, "You are my father," and to a stone, "You gave me birth"(2:26-27). According to Bright, the tree and stone symbolized the gods of fertility, and they believed that their own existence came from the gods.[13] Thus, they worshiped them and prayed to them. This is serious corruption. However, Judah did not care about the results of this fall. The phrase, "Judah did not fear" means that Judah did not take their sin seriously and took no heed to the judgment following their adulteries and harlotry. The Hebrew word $bāgôḏā$ (בגודה) means to "act treacherously" or "faithless" and is used for Judah, the adulterer. This term is used for both marriage and covenants. In the context of marriage, it is used for the one who breaks the marriage relationship and begins a new relationship with another man.[14] In the context of a covenant, the term is used for the one who has violated the covenantal obligations. The treacherousness of Judah was intentional and deliberate. They defiled the land by their adulteries and did not return to YHWH. Since Israel was driven out of the land and taken into captivity by Assyria because of their treacherous acts, Judah will also face the same fate. Judah will be driven out and given a writ of divorce and taken to Babylon. YHWH pronounces the fate of Judah in view of Israel's fall.

(3) Jeremiah 31:31-34

Jeremiah 31 begins with the covenant formula. "At that time I will be the God

---

13. John Bright, *Jeremiah*,16, 24
14. P. C. Craigie, 55-66.

of all the families of Israel and they shall be my people." This formula is also found in 30:22. "At that time" refers to the time when YHWH will bring the remnants of Israel from the northern countries and gather them from the remote parts of the earth (8). It will be the time of restoration. At that time YHWH will restore and renew the relationship with Israel. Accordingly, this covenant does not refer to the past one, but a future one. YHWH distinguishes the differences between the past and future ones.

31   "Behold, days are coming," declares YHWH, "when I will make a new covenant with the house of Israel and with the house of Judah,
32   not like the covenant which I made with their fathers in the day I took them by the hand to bring them out of the land of Egypt, my covenant which they broke, although I was a husband to them, declares YHWH.
33   "But this is the covenant which I will make with the house of Israel after those days," declares YHWH, "I will put my law within them, and on their heart I will write it; and I will be their God, and they shall be my people."
34   "And they shall not teach again, each man his neighbor and each man his brother, saying, 'Know YHWH,' for they shall all know me, from the least of them to the greatest of them," declares YHWH, "for I will forgive their iniquity, and their sin I will remember no more."

YHWH is going to make a new covenant with Israel. In contrast to this new covenant, the old covenant is the one that he made with their fathers on the day he took them by the hand to bring them out of the land of Egypt (32). The covenant he made with Israel on the day of the exodus is the Sinai covenant. The old covenant or the Sinai covenant is the past one and is now broken. YHWH recalled the day the covenant was made with Israel and said, "My covenant which they broke, although I was a husband to them." According to this phrase, YHWH made a covenant with Israel as a husband at Mount Sinai. Thus, Israel is viewed as the wife of YHWH. And the covenant ceremony on the mount can be regarded as a wedding between YHWH and Israel, since marriage was a contract between spouses in the ancient Near East. According to Jeremiah's theological insight, the Sinai covenant was YHWH's wedding with Israel. Whereas Jeremiah described Israel's journey after the exodus through the wilderness under YHWH's guidance as "the love of betrothal" in 2:2, he understood the covenant on Mount Sinai as a wedding. Unfortunately the marriage covenant had been broken because of Israel's apostasy. The Sinai covenant is the broken covenant. Thus, YHWH is going to make a new covenant with Israel.

The Marriage Texts

The new covenant will be fundamentally different from the old one. The Sinai covenant was engraved on stone and was put in the holy of holies in the temple. But the new covenant will be engraved upon the heart of man and will not be erased or broken forever. The new covenant will be established on the basis of YHWH's full forgiveness for her past adulteries. Israel's relationship with YHWH and her knowledge of him will be so perfect and full that the exhortation to know him will no longer be necessary. On the day that YHWH establishes the new covenant with Israel, he will again proclaim the covenant formula, "I will be their God and they shall be my people," which obviously originated from the marriage formula.[15] The marriage and covenant between YHWH and Israel carry similar points in their concept and nature. The basic nature of a marriage and a covenant is a relationship. The focal point of the new covenant is also about establishing a new relationship. The new covenant that YHWH is going to make with Israel will be stronger than a human marriage which can easily be broken. It will be a more perfect and intimate relationship.

To this point it has been observed that Jeremiah understood the YHWH-Israel relationship from the perspective of a marriage between a husband and wife. For him the exodus was viewed as an engagement, the covenant of Mount Sinai as a wedding, Israel's religious apostasy as adultery, and the following fall and exile as a divorce. However, viewing the restoration of Israel as a remarriage in Jeremiah is not as clear as it was in Hosea and Ezekiel. Jeremiah describes it as a new covenant.

There are a few similar points between the marriage metaphor of Hosea and Jeremiah. First of all, Hosea mainly dealt with Israel's religious apostasy before the fall of Samaria in terms of the marriage metaphor. However, Jeremiah used the marriage metaphor to waken Judah and warn her not to follow Israel's way of apostasy which led to the fall of the nation and their ensuing deportation. Thus it was didactic in nature. Secondly, Hosea describes YHWH as a husband who pursued his adulterous wife and married her again, but Jeremiah put more emphasis on the imagery of YHWH who is

---

15 Seock-Tae Sohn, "'I Will Be Your God and You Will Be My People': The Origin and Background of the Covenant Formula" *Ki Baruch Hu: Ancient Near Eastern, Biblical, and Judaic Studies in Honor of Baruch A. Levine.* R. Chazan, W. W. Hallo, L. H. Schiffman, eds. (Winona Lake: Eisenbrauns, 1999), 355-372.

waiting for Israel's return. Thirdly, both Hosea and Jeremiah emphasize the restoration of Israel. For them the reason for the restoration is to establish a new covenant relationship. Hosea sees the restoration as YHWH's remarriage with Israel in righteousness, justice, lovingkindness and compassion as he makes his dwelling among them forever. Jeremiah understands it in terms of YHWH making a new covenant which is different from that made at Mount Sinai. The new covenant will be based on his forgiveness of their sins and will be engraved in the heart of man and will never be broken forever. Their relationship will be more perfect, solid and stronger than that of a husband-wife. Whereas Hosea puts more emphasis on the emotional side, Jeremiah focuses on the legal side.

3. THE BOOK OF EEZEKIEL

A. Ezekiel 16:1-63

It seems to be obvious that Hosea is the first one who described the YHWH-Israel relation in terms of a husband-wife relationship. We can find such parables and metaphors in other texts, too, but Hosea seems to be the first one to formulate the theological concept, put it into a metaphor and write it down using a series of life events such as the marriage, divorce, and remarriage of a couple. The metaphor of marriage was widely known to the kingdoms of both Israel and Judah from ancient times. This metaphor was refined and supplemented through the history of Israel so that it became perfected by the hand of Ezekiel. He used Hosea's metaphor and expanded it in detail to fit in the context of the exile. The following is an outline of Ezek. 16.

(1) The birth of Jerusalem (1-5)
(2) The marriage of Jerusalem (6-14)
(3) The adultery of Jerusalem (15-34)
(4) The rejection of Jerusalem (35-59)
(5) The restoration of Jerusalem (60-63)

It is to be noted that the spouse of YHWH in Ezek. 16 is not Israel, but the city of Jerusalem. However, it is clear that Jerusalem symbolizes the inhabitants of the city, or the nation of Israel.[16] The text begins with YHWH taking an abandoned girl by the road and bringing her up as a daughter, which symbolizes the city of Jerusalem as well as the people of Israel.

(1) The Birth of Jerusalem (16:1-5)

The first paragraph of Ezek 16 is about the origin and background of Israel, designated here as Jerusalem.

1 Then the word of YHWH came to me saying,
2 Son of man, make known to Jerusalem her abominations,
3 and say, 'Thus says YHWH God to Jerusalem, "Your origin and your birth are from the land of the Canaanites, your father was an Amorite and your mother a Hittite.
4 "As for your birth, on the day you were born your navel cord was not cut, nor were you washed with water for cleansing; you were not rubbed with salt or even wrapped in cloths.
5 "No eye looked with pity on you to do any of these things for you, to have compassion on you. Rather you were thrown out into the open field, for you were abhorred on the day you were born.

The tragic story of a girl abandoned in an open field after her birth begins with her family background. The birthplace of the girl named Jerusalem was Canaan. Her father was an Amorite and her mother was a Hittite. This does not mean that the forefathers of Israel referred to here as Jerusalem came from the Amorites and Hittites. According to the list of nations in Ex. 5:8; 23:23, the Amorites were one of the nations settled in Canaan. They belonged

---

16. Moshe Greenberg, *Ezekiel 1-20*, 274. John B. Taylor, *Ezekiel* (TOTC 16 ; Leicester: IVP, 1969),133. G. A. Cooke, *Ezekiel* (ICC; Edinburgh: T. & T. Clark, 1972), 159. However, Brownlee says that the phrases about the birth of Jerusalem are historically correct in describing the origin of Jerusalem in Canaan and they refer to the city itself. William H. Brownlee, *Ezekiel 1-19*, 223-24. Lately Galambush has also proposed the same opinion as Brownlee. Julie Galambush, *Jerusalem in the Book of Ezekiel: The City as Yahweh's Wife* (SBL Dissertation Series 130; Atlanta: Scholars Press, 1992). However, God made his covenant with man, not with a city, as Greenberg pointed out. Furthermore, if we interpret Jerusalem as the people of Israel, the metaphor fits in well with the situation of Israel.

to the Northwest Semites and are known to have lived in the Near East from the second millennium B.C. As a nomadic people, they invaded Babylon and established an empire. At the time of Israel's arrival in Canaan they occupied almost all the area of the east of the Jordan. The defeat of Sihon and Og made it easy for Israel to conquer the land of Canaan. The Hittites were from the Indo-European family and the major stage of their life activity was Asia Minor. However, some of them migrated to the northern part of Canaan and controlled all the area until Israel's arrival.[17] The Amorites and the Hittites were simply one of the seven ethnic groups who inhabited the land of Canaan before Israel's conquest.

Accordingly, the Amorite and Hittite origin of Israel is a metaphorical description and simply means that the status of Israel before YHWH's election of Israel as his people was basically the same as that of an Amorite, or Hittite who had nothing to do with him. Israel was like a child deserted by her parents in an open field. In the ancient world the practice of abandoning an unwanted child on the roadside at its birth was socially acceptable. Parents did this with the expectation that a passerby might find the infant and take pity on it and bring it up as his own, rather than simply leaving it to die. Moses' story in the Old Testament (Ex. 2:1-10), the story of Sargon of Agade who reigned about 2360 B.C. (*ANET*, 119), Herodotus' story of the exposure of Cyrus (I. 107-17), Diodorus Siculus' story of Agothacles of Syracuse (XIX.2. 4-7) and the legend of Romulus and Remus who built Rome, etc. all have a similar story.[18]

In verse 4, four negative clauses describe actions which the mother of the infant, Jerusalem, should have taken at the time of the infant's birth. For a newborn infant, the navel cord was to be cut; its body was to be washed with water, rubbed with salt and wrapped in cloths. Rubbing with salt was for sanitary purposes. In ancient Palestine, they applied not only salt, but also oil. Masterman describes the Palestinian custom as follows:

> As soon as the navel is cut the midwife rubs the child all over with salt, water, and oil and tightly swathes it in clothes for seven days; at the end of that time

17. H. A. Hoffner, "Some Contributions of Hittitology to Old Testament Study," *Tyndale Bulletin* XX (1969): 27 ff.
18. Brownlee, 222.

The Marriage Texts

she removes the dirty clothes, washes the child and anoints it, and then wraps it up again for seven days and so on till the fortieth day.[19]

However, nothing was done for this deserted baby. Immediately after its birth the parents threw the infant away into the open field, not by the roadside. If it were deserted by the roadside, a passer-by would have found it and rescued it. But the parent of this newborn infant had not taken this into account. Its fate was entirely in the hands of God. If the status of Israel before YHWH took her as his people is like a girl abandoned in an open field, its fate can be compared to a wounded reed or a candle before the wind. Israel had no glory before she was chosen by YHWH.

(2) The Marriage of Jerusalem (16:6-14)

The second paragraph of Ezek. 16 tells of YHWH taking the abandoned infant as his daughter and eventually taking her as his wife.

6   "When I passed by you and saw you squirming in your blood, I said to you while you were in your blood, 'Live!' I said to you while you were in your blood, 'Live!'

7   "I made you numerous like plants of the field. Then you grew up, became tall, and reached the age for fine ornaments; your breasts were formed and your hair had grown. Yet you were naked and bare.

8   "Then I passed by you and saw you, and behold, you were at the time for love; so I spread my skirt over you and covered your nakedness. I also swore to you and entered into a covenant with you so that you became mine," declares the Lord YHWH.

9   "Then I bathed you with water, washed off your blood from you, and anointed you with oil.

10   "I also clothed you with embroidered cloth, and put sandals of porpoise skin on your feet; and I wrapped you with fine linen and covered you with silk.

11   "And I adorned you with ornaments, put bracelets on your hands, and a necklace around your neck.

12   "I also put a ring in your nostril, earrings in your ears, and a beautiful crown on your head.

---

19. E. W. G. Masterman, "Hygiene and Disease in Palestine," *PEFQ* 50 (1918):118-19. quoted by Brownlee, 223.

13 "Thus you were adorned with gold and silver, and your dress was of fine linen, silk, and embroidered cloth. You ate fine flour, honey, and oil; so you were exceedingly beautiful and advanced to royalty.
14 "Then your fame went forth among the nations on account of your beauty, for it was perfect because of my splendor which I bestowed on you," declares the Lord YHWH.

YHWH found the deserted infant squirming in her own blood as he passed by. She was still alive and fluttering her feet instinctively. YHWH said to her, "Live! Live!" He made her live by the power of his divine voice. He then brought her up and she became numerous like plants of the field. The expression, "numerous like plants of the field" refers to Israel's growth in number as a result of his care. More than the growth in numbers, the child became tall and reached the age for fine ornaments, and her breasts were formed and hair had grown. The girl became a mature woman. The Hebrew phrase, *ba'aḏî 'aḏîm* (בעדי עדיים) rendered as "fine ornament," means literally "ornament of ornaments." It thus describes the most beautiful appearance possible.[20] The "hair" mentioned here seems to refer to pubic hair.[21] Though the girl had fully matured, yet she was naked and bare (7). According to ancient custom, if a man wanted to marry a girl, he would spread or throw his clothes over her.[22] A similar case is found in verse 8. YHWH said that he spread his skirt over her and covered her nakedness. In view of this custom, the expression "Yet you were naked and bare" means that no one had yet taken her as his wife even though she was mature enough to get married.

YHWH again passed by her and saw her and found that she was at the time for love. He thus claimed her for marriage. He then swore to her and entered into a covenant with her so that she became his (8). The Hebrew *'eṯ doḏîm* (עת דדים), translated as "the time for love," means the age of sexual lovemaking (Ezek. 23:17; Prov. 7:16; SS 4:10; 7:13). Swearing and making a covenant are very important elements in the process of marriage. Therefore, "I swear to you and entered into a covenant with you" in verse 8 means that

---

20. However, some scholars have emended the text as ותבאי בעת עדים and translated it as "she began to undergo menstruation." Zimmerli, 324. Cooke, 163. Taylor, 135.

21. Greenberg, 276.

22. We can find this custom not only in Israel (Ruth 3:9; Mishnah Peah 4:3), but also in ancient Arabia. Greenberg, 277. Raphael Patai, *Sex and Family in the Bible and the Middle East* (Garden City: Doubleday, 1959), 97.

YHWH was married to Israel. Further, YHWH said that she became his. As has been noted above, marriage in the ancient world basically carried the concept of possession. YHWH took possession of her by marriage. All these phrases and expressions describe the YHWH-Israel relationship in terms of human marriage and the Sinai covenant of YHWH with Israel in terms of a wedding, which is also found in Jeremiah.

Verses 9-14 describe YHWH's lavish efforts to make his bride bright and happy. The girl became a queen since she married YHWH, the king of kings. YHWH brought her into his house and washed, anointed, and clothed her. The blood washed off from her seems to refer to her virginal bleeding caused by the first coitus. The bride saved the bloodstained garment or bed sheet as proof of her virginity at the time of her marriage.[23] Anointing naturally followed a bath. The groom clothed her with embroidered cloth and dressed her in fine linen, covering her with costly garments (10). He put leather sandals on her. He adorned her with precious jewelry for her hands, around her neck, in her nostrils and ears. He even put a beautiful crown on her head (11-12). Furthermore, he provided her with fine flour, honey, and oil so that she became very beautiful and rose to be a queen. YHWH bestowed his splendor on her and her beauty was perfect (14). Now her fame spread among the nations on account of her beauty. She owed her life, her marriage, her wealth and beauty etc. all to YHWH who chose her as his wife. She had no merit to deserve such an honor.

Before she was taken by YHWH as his people, Israel was like a deserted infant in an open field. But he brought her up and took her as his people so that she acquired a new status. She became a queen and enjoyed all kinds of privileges and riches. She was not qualified or deserving to be his people (Deut. 7:7 ff; 9:4 ff; 32:10; Jer. 2:2; Hos. 9:10). Only by the grace and good will of YHWH was she chosen and became his people. Israel's fame and news of her beauty went out to all the world because she was his people. Historically Hosea seems to have in mind the period of David and Solomon when he mentioned the riches and glory of Jerusalem.

(3) The Adultery of Jerusalem (16:15-34)

Jerusalem was not faithful to her spouse. She played the harlot. The third paragraph of Ezek. 16 describes the behavior of her playing the harlot with all the passersby. Verses 15-22 portray Jerusalem's apostasy in terms of the metaphor of her playing the harlot with passersby, but verses 23-29 depict Jerusalem's military dependence upon the gentile nations in terms of her playing the harlot with gentiles. Verses 30-34 describe the peculiar way Jerusalem played the harlot. She gave money to men rather than receiving payment from them.

a. Jerusalem's religious adultery (16:15-22)

15 "But you trusted in your beauty and played the harlot because of your fame, and you poured out your harlotries on every passer-by who might be willing.
16 "And you took some of your clothes, made for yourself high places of various colors, and played the harlot on them, which should never come about nor happen.
17 "You also took your beautiful jewels made of my gold and of my silver, which I had given you, and made for yourself male images that you might play the harlot with them.
18 "Then you took your embroidered cloth and covered them, and offered my oil and my incense before them.
19 "Also my bread which I gave you, fine flour, oil, and honey with which I fed you, you would offer before them for a soothing aroma; so it happened," declares the Lord YHWH.
20 "Moreover, you took your sons and daughters whom you have borne to me, and you sacrificed them to idols to be devoured. Were your harlotries so small a matter?
22 "You slaughtered my children, and offered them up to idols by causing them to pass through the fire.
22 "And besides all your abominations and harlotries, you did not remember the days of your youth, when you were naked and bare and squirming in your blood.

Jerusalem trusted in her beauty instead of her God. She behaved as though all her beauty and fame were her own and made use of them for playing the harlot. She poured out her harlotry on every passerby and was possessed by them.[24] YHWH regards Israel's playing the harlot as the one thing "which should never come about nor happen" (16) because they made high places of various colors with the clothes he had given her (16), male images with the gold and silver he had given (17), and before idols, they offered the oil, incense, bread, fine flour and honey which YHWH had given to Israel to feed her (18, 19). Moreover, Israel slaughtered her children whom she had borne to YHWH and sacrificed them to the idols (20, 21).

The Hebrew *bamôṭ* (במות) was a sanctuary or temple built on a mountain. According to Albright, its origin was a stone pile or a stone pillar erected by a tomb in memory of the dead.[25] The people of Israel sacrificed in this place under the direction of a local priest until the temple was built. Samuel blessed the sacrifice on the high place of Ramah (1Sam. 9:12-13). Solomon went up to Gibeon and offered sacrifices and burnt offerings on the high place there (1Kgs. 3:4). However, once the temple was built, offering sacrifices on the high places was prohibited. After the schism of the kingdom, Jeroboam, king of the northern kingdom, built an altar at Bethel and Dan corresponding to the temple of Jerusalem. From that time on, it was almost impossible to control the sacrifices on the high places. Influenced by ancestor worship, the fertility cult, and various other forms of idol worship, they offered sacrifices and made feasts on this place. The "high places of various colors" in verse 16 seems to refer to a curtain woven from a variety of colorful threads and drawn to a tent. There is a record that the women of Judah wove hangings for Asherah in 2 Kgs. 23:7. In this context the people of Israel decorated the high places with clothes which YHWH had given to them.

YHWH classified the adultery of Jerusalem as the one thing which "should never come about nor happen"(16), because she offered to the idols the gifts such as various jewels and clothes and food which he had given to her. Further, she betrayed and rebelled against him by giving her mind and body and possessions to her lover, not to her husband who had given her all

---

24. Variant readings of MT לו־יהי (it became his) have been proposed. The NASB reading of "who might be willing" does not express the meaning of the context. Though the rendering of "it became his" is not fully accorded with literal meaning, it reflects the marriage formula and the idea of possession is implied in it. Cf. Greenberg, 280.

25. W. F. Albright, "The High Place in Ancient Palestine" in *Volume de Congrès, Strasbourg 1956*, VT Supp. 4 (Leiden, 1957): 242-58.

kinds of beautiful gifts as a token of his love and marriage. Among her disgusting behaviors, the practice of offering human sacrifices to other gods was the most abominable practice which provoked YHWH's anger. She took her sons and daughters whom she had borne to YHWH and sacrificed them as food to idols (20). The phrase "causing them to pass through the fire" in verse 20 is not simply passing through a fire. It was slaughtering her children and burning them on the fire and offering them to the idols, Molech and Baal. This kind of detestable practice was done by Ahaz (2 Kgs 16:13) and Mannasseh (2 Kgs 21:6), the kings of Judah (Jer. 7:31; 19:5). Jerusalem forgot her miserable origins when she was deserted in an open field at her birth and YHWH who saved her life, brought her up, took her as his wife and gave her riches and honor. She betrayed YHWH her husband.

b. Jerusalem's military adultery (16:23-29)

The previous paragraphs dealt with Jerusalem's adultery from the perspective of religious apostasy, but this section details her military dependence on others besides YHWH. He regards Jerusalem's dependence on neighboring powers and her requests for military aid from those other than YHWH in times of crisis of existence as an apostasy betraying her lord and husband.

23 "Then it came about after all your wickedness ('Woe, woe to you!' declares the Lord YHWH),
24 that you built yourself a shrine and made yourself a high place in every square.
25 "You built yourself a high place at the top of every street, and made your beauty abominable; and you spread your legs to every passer-by to multiply your harlotry.
26 "You also played the harlot with the Egyptians, your lustful neighbors, and multiplied your harlotry to make me angry.
27 "Behold now, I have stretched out my hand against you and diminished your rations. And I delivered you up to the desire of those who hate you, the daughters of the Philistines, who are ashamed of your lewd conduct.
28 "Moreover, you played the harlot with the Assyrians because you were not satisfied; you even played the harlot with them and still were not satisfied.
29 "You also multiplied your harlotry with the land of merchants, Chaldea, yet even with this you were not satisfied."

The Marriage Texts

Jerusalem is said to have built a shrine, a high place, at the top of every street and she spread her legs to every passerby to play her harlotry. The Hebrew words *geḇ* (גב, shrine) and *rāmā* (רמה, a high places) are commonly used as synonyms for "high place" (16) and seem to be roof-top shrines which were situated at strategic and commanding positions at the intersections of city streets. These places seem to have been used not simply for commercial prostitution, but for fertility rites in connection with the Canaanite religion.[26] The expression, "to spread one's legs" is a euphemism for the sexual posture of a woman or her self-exposure.

Jerusalem's partners in her adultery were Egypt, Assyria, and Babylon. These nations were situated on the northern and southern borders of Israel, and from time to time threatened and invaded her borders. When Egypt advanced over the southern border to invade her, Jerusalem asked for military aid from the north, and when Assyria and Babylon threatened the northern border, she tried to depend upon the southern armies for help.

Ahaz, the king of Jerusalem, asked for military aid from Tiglath-pileser, the king of Assyria, and became his vassal when Pekah of Samaria and Rezin of Syria made a military coalition and invaded Judah. Zedekiah, the last king of Jerusalem, asked for military help from Egypt in order to be independent from the Babylonian rule of Nebuchadnezzar (Jer. 37:3-5; Ezek. 17:13-17). However, this brought about her downfall in the end (2 Kgs. 21:1-21; Jer. 52:1-11). Jerusalem chose Chaldea as her last partner for adultery in verse 29. This verse refers to Babylon and "the land of merchants." In the Bible this primarily referred to the land of Canaan where the Phoenicians, having a good sense of trade, dwelt (Gen. 10:15; Hos. 12:8; Zeph. 1:11; Zech. 14:21; Prov. 31:24).[27] However, in this verse and in Ezek. 17:4 Babylon is called "the land of merchants."

YHWH is the husband of Jerusalem. Thus she had to ask for his help and depend only upon him for her security in times of national crisis caused by the invasion of other nations. However, she did not trust him. If any nation asked for military aid from another nation in the ancient world, it meant that

---

26. Taylor,138. However, some proposed it was a place used for professional prostitutes. Greenberg, 281-82.

27. M. Astour, "The Origin of the Terms 'Canaan,' 'Phoenician,' and 'Purple,'" *JNES* 24 (1965): 346 ff. Greenberg, 283-84.

the nation herself would become a vassal of the other nation and became a servant of the suzerain's gods. They had to worship and serve the gods of their suzerain. When Ahaz survived the Syro-Ephramite threat with the help of Tiglath-pileser, he went to the temple in Damascus and worshiped the gods of Tiglath-pileser. When he returned from Damascus, he remodeled the temple of YHWH in Jerusalem according to the pattern of the one in Damascus, and he worshiped and offered various sacrifices every morning and evening as in Damascus (2 Kgs. 16:5-20). In the ancient world, politics and military affairs were tightly related to religion, and it was almost impossible to separate one from the other. They were organically tied together. Thus it was possible to describe Jerusalem's military dependence on other nations rather than YHWH in terms of adultery.

The Egyptians are designated as $\check{s}^e k\bar{e}nayi\underline{k}\ gi\underline{d}l\hat{e}\ b\bar{a}\check{s}ar$ (שכניך גדלי בשר , your neighbor of big flesh) in verse 26. The literal meaning of $b\bar{a}\check{s}ar$ (בשר) is "flesh," "skin," "sacrificial meat." According to Gen. 17:13 and Lev. 15:2 ff, we can see it is used as a euphemistic expression for a man's sexual organ. Particularly, the description of the Egyptians as a neighbor of big flesh means that they had the ability to satisfy the sexual desire of the lewd Israel. The description of the Philistines in verse 27 as the ones who hated Israel seems to take into account their rival attempts to take leadership in controlling the Palestinian region throughout their history. Thus, the Philistines are portrayed as Israel's female rival, not as a male partner with whom she played the harlot. During the period of Ahaz' reign in Judah, "the Philistines also invaded the cities of the lowland and the Negev of Judah, and had taken Beth-shemesh, Aijalan. Gederoth, and Soco with its villages, Timnah with its villages, and Gimzo with its villages, and they settled there." (2 Ch. 28:18). After Sennacherib suppressed the Palestinian revolt and won the victory, he handed over Ashdot, Eglon, and Gaza of Judah to the Philistines.[28] The phrase, "I delivered you up to the desire of those who hate you, the daughters of the Philistines," in verse 27 seems to refer to this incident.

Jerusalem played the harlot with her neighboring countries in the area of

---

28. *ANET*, 288a. O. Eissfeldt, *Palastina-Jahrbuch* 27 (1931): 58-66 [=Klein Schriften I, 239-46.] "His (Hezekiah's) towns which I had despoiled I cut off from his land, giving them Mitinti, king of Ashdod, Padi, king of Ekron, and Sillibel, king of Gaza, and reduced his land" (*DOTT*, 67).

national security. Because of this, YHWH disciplined her with a severe whip, but she never stopped playing the harlot. In verses 28 and 29, the phrases expressing Israel's dissatisfaction, such as " . . . because you were not satisfied; you even played the harlot with them and still were not satisfied . . . yet even with this you were not satisfied," are repeated. This represents Israel's unceasing dependence upon the big powers around her in terms of the dissatisfied harlots sitting in the streets to seduce the passersby. The harlotry of Jerusalem was dissatisfying and never ceasing, a kind of burning fire, never extinguished or put out.

c. *Jerusalem's peculiar adultery (16:30-34)*

YHWH introduces another peculiar type of adultery here in Ezek. 16:30-34.

30 "How languishing is your heart," declares YHWH the Lord, "while you do all these things, the actions of a bold-faced harlot.
31 "When you built your shrine at the beginning of every street and made your high place in every square, in disdaining money, you were not like a harlot.
32 "You adulteress wife, who takes strangers instead of her husband!
33 "Men give gifts to all harlots, but you give your gifts to all your lovers to bribe them to come to you from every direction for your harlotries.
34 "Thus you are different from those women in your harlotries, in that no one plays the harlot as you do, because you give money andno money is given you; thus you are different."

The difference between the harlotry of Jerusalem and that of others is that women usually take money when playing the harlot, but Jerusalem paid for her harlotry. Men give gifts to all harlots, but she gave her gifts to all her lovers to bribe them to come to her from every direction for her harlotry. The reason for this is that no one came to her. Once men came to her from all over the world because of her fame and beauty. However, her splendor and beauty have now faded away. She became old and had nothing left to attract men and to hold their eyes upon her. Her life as a harlot was almost at the point of death. Nevertheless, she could not control her sexual desire and seduced men to seek her by giving them money and gifts. Obviously this was absurd, because she had already invested too much for her professional harlotry. She built herself a shrine and made herself a high place in every square and at the top of every street. Instead of recovering the cost, she still gave her money away. Her purpose in playing the harlots seems not to be in making money, but in seeking carnal pleasure. The Hebrew expression *mā ʾamulā libṭêk* (מה אמלה לבתך) in verse 30 is in accord with her passion, since "How hot your ardor is" is a much better rendering than that of the NASB's "How languishing is your heart."[29] Moreover, in verse 32, she is called an "adulteress wife, who takes strangers instead of her husband."

Ahaz, king of Judah, gave the gold and silver stored at the temple and his palace to Tiglath-pileser and asked for his military aid when the Syro-Ephramite coalition invaded (2 Kgs.16:8). The Assyrian king accepted them and rescued her. Again Hezekiah, king of Judah, also gave all the silver in the temple and palace to Sennacherib as he attacked the cities of Judah, even cutting off the gold from the doors of the temple and from the door posts (2 Kgs.18:13-16). Thus, Jerusalem was dependent upon the neighboring countries for her national security, not upon YHWH her husband. Ezekiel portrays Judah's dependency on her neighbor's power as a peculiar type of adultery.

(4) The Judgment on Jerusalem (16:35-59)

YHWH exposed and explained the sins of Israel, designated as Jerusalem, using the metaphor of a husband and wife through the mouth of Ezekiel. Now it is time to give a ruling on their behavior. This section (35-59) is composed of two paragraphs. The first one describes YHWH's punishment of the adulterous wife through her lover (35-43), and the second one depicts YHWH disgracing Jerusalem through Sodom and Samaria (44-59). YHWH's punishment is very simple. He had Jerusalem betrayed and destroyed by her lover whom she had loved and to whom she had given her body and money. Further, he had her disgraced by saving and elevating her enemy and by erasing the distinction between Israel and the gentiles, between the elect and non-elect.

---

29. Cf. Greenberg, 383.

The Marriage Texts

a. *YHWH punishes his adulterous wife through her lovers (Ezek. 16:35-43)*

35 Therefore, O harlot, hear the word of YHWH.
36 Thus says YHWH GOD, "Because your lewdness was poured out and your nakedness uncovered through your harlotries with your lovers and with all your detestable idols, and because of the blood of your sons which you gave to idols,
37 therefore, behold, I shall gather all your lovers with whom you took pleasure, even all those whom you loved and all those whom you hated. So I shall gather them against you from every direction and expose your nakedness to them that they may see all your nakedness.
38 "Thus I shall judge you, like women who commit adultery or shed blood are judged; and I shall bring on you the blood of wrath and jealousy.
39 "I shall also give you into the hands of your lovers, and they will tear down your shrines, demolish your high places, strip you of your clothing, take away your jewels, and will leave you naked and bare.
40 "They will incite a crowd against you, and they will stone you and cut you to pieces with their swords.
41 "And they will burn your houses with fire and execute judgments on you in the sight of many women. Then I shall stop you from playing the harlot, and you will also no longer pay your lovers.
42 "So I shall calm my fury against you, and my jealousy will depart from you, and I shall be pacified and angry no more.
43 "Because you have not remembered the days of your youth but have enraged me by all these things, behold, I in turn will bring your conduct down on your own head," declares YHWH GOD, "so that you will not commit this lewdness on top of all your other abominations.

YHWH burned with jealousy and anger and had no peace because of Jerusalem's adultery (42). He is going to pour out his judgment upon her. Thus, it begins with "O harlot, hear the word of YHWH"(35). The abominable crime of Jerusalem was to give the blood of her sons to idols. The NASB's rendering of the Hebrew $n^e\d{h}\={o}\v{s}^et$ (נחשת) as "lewdness" is not clear here. According to Greenberg, $n^e\d{h}\={o}\v{s}^et$ (נחשת) came from the Akkadian cognate $n\d{h}\v{s}$ (to be abundant, overflowing) and its derivative $na\d{h}a\v{s}ati$ refers to a genital overflow of a woman when she is in heat.[30] The term *šāpak* (שפך) describes the pouring out of water, or raining in buckets. Thus, "your lewdness was poured out" (36) seems to be an expression that reminds us of animals calling their mating spouses at breeding season. Jerusalem was seen in the eyes of YHWH as such animals seeking their partners. Jerusalem poured out her lewdness and uncovered her nakedness by playing the harlot with her lover.

YHWH's principle of punishment is to bring their conduct down on their own head (42). YHWH will gather all of Jerusalem's lovers with whom she took pleasure and all those whom she hated from every direction of the world and will have them attack her. He will strip her in front of them that they may all see her nakedness. He will bring her into his court. He will sentence her to the punishment of a woman who has committed adultery and who has shed blood. He will bring upon her the blood vengeance of his wrath and jealous anger. In the end he will hand her over to her lovers. Then they will bring a mob against her and stone her and hack her down to pieces with swords. After this the wrath of YHWH against her will subside and his jealous anger will dissipate and he will be calm and no longer angry.

What does this figurative description mean? It refers to the forthcoming destruction of Jerusalem. The neighboring countries of Judah on which she depended for military assistance will invade Jerusalem and tear down the mound and destroy the lofty shrines. They will strip the people of Jerusalem of her clothes and take her fine jewelry. They will burn down her houses and demolish the entire city. Historically, the northern kingdom was destroyed by Assyria and the southern kingdom by Babylon. The people of Israel were taken captive to Babylon, and some of them escaped to Egypt. However, they were oppressed and scorned and had to suffer forced labor. Israel became a captive and was stripped and whipped. Zedekiah, the last king of Judah, was taken to Babylon, and his sons were slaughtered before him. Even his eyes were plucked out. The countries such as Assyria, Babylon and Moab etc. whom Israel once loved or hated were the agents YHWH was going to use to destroy the city. Since YHWH suffered betrayal by Israel, he in return had her betrayed and suffer at the hands of her lovers whom she loved and to whom she gave money and gifts and even sacrificed her children. Furthermore, he put a stone and knife in the hands of her lovers and committed her to them for

---

30. Ibid., 28-56.

The Marriage Texts

execution. For this reason, YHWH called Assyria "the staff of my indignation" in Isaiah (Isa. 10:5), and Nebuchadnezzar, king of Babylon, "my servant," was chosen to punish Israel in Jeremiah (Jer. 25:8-11). As an upstart would often forget his former days of poverty, Israel forgot her birth and early days and enacted all kinds of evil against her husband. Thus he is going to bring her conduct down on her own head (43). YHWH, however, did not kill her. Through this vengeance, he appeases his anger and jealousy on the one hand, and he stops her from playing the harlot and worshiping idols on the other hand.

b. YHWH humiliating Jerusalem through Sodom and Samaria (16:44-59)

YHWH pronounces two kinds of judgements on Israel. One is physical punishment. He exposes Israel's nakedness before her lovers and had them stone her. The other one is to restore and elevate the fate of her neighbors which she looked down on and to treat them as he did Jerusalem; thus, her privileges as his chosen people are taken away. No distinction can be found between Jerusalem and the other neighboring cities. It is a kind of humiliation for Jerusalem. There will be a day of restoration for Sodom and Samaria and Jerusalem, but this will bring nothing but shame and humiliation for Jerusalem. In this section, the following can be observed: (1) Jerusalem justifying Sodom and Samaria (44-52), (2) Sodom and Samaria being a comfort to Jerusalem (53-59).

a) Jerusalem justifying Sodom and Samaria (16:44-52)

48 "As I live," declares the Lord YHWH, "Sodom, your sister, and her daughters, have not done as you and your daughters have done.
49 "Behold, this was the guilt of your sister Sodom: she and her daughters had arrogance, abundant food, and careless ease, but she did not help the poor and needy.
50 Thus they were haughty and committed abominations before me. Therefore I removed them when I saw it.

51 "Furthermore, Samaria did not commit half of your sins, for you have multiplied your abominations more than they. Thus you have made your sisters appear righteous by all your abominations which you have committed.

52 "Also bear your disgrace in that you have made judgment favorable for your sisters. Because of your sins in which you acted more abominably than they, they are more in the right than you. Yes, be also ashamed and bear your disgrace, in that you made your sisters appear righteous.

The judgement of YHWH on Jerusalem begins with a popular proverb, "Like mother, like daughter"(44). He introduces the family of Jerusalem and her sins. Her mother was a Hittite, her father an Amorite, the elder sister was Samaria living north of her, and her younger sister was Sodom living south of her. YHWH indicts her mother and elder sister as the ones who loathed their husbands and children. Jerusalem follows their immoral and unethical practices of idol worship. The Hittites and Amorites had settled in the land of Canaan before Israel arrived there. Leviticus lists the abominable practices among the Hittites and Amorites of their sexual life and the sacrificing of their children to Molech and commanded, "Do not defile yourselves by any of these things; for by all these the nations which I am casting out before you have become defiled"(Lev. 18:24). Again in Lev. 20:23 YHWH said, "You shall not follow the customs of the nation which I shall drive out before you, for they did all these things, and therefore I abhorred them." From these prohibitions it can be deduced that the abominable deed of Israel's "loathing her husband and children" was enacted by and learned from the former inhabitants of the land.

Samaria and Sodom are portrayed as sisters. Samaria is the elder sister and Sodom the younger one. Historically Samaria came into existence after Jerusalem, and Sodom began before Jerusalem. Thus the distinction between the elder and younger was not made according to their age. Rather it was made according to their size. Since Samaria was bigger than Judah, it was called the elder sister, and since Sodom was smaller than Judah she was the younger. Again Samaria is referred to as the one "who lives north of you with her daughters"(46) and Sodom as the one "who lives south of you, with her daughters." Jerusalem is the center and standard for taking the directions of north and south. The term, "daughters" is used for the satellite villages around a big city. These villages were dependent upon the mother city in various ways. The villagers would go to the city and enjoy special occasions with the people in the city in the festival seasons, or they could find security in the city in time of war. Thus, "the daughters of Samaria" and "the daughters of Sodom" refer to those villages around Samaria and Sodom.

Unfortunately, Samaria and Sodom are the cities that YHWH punished because of their sins and rebellion. Sodom was arrogant with her abundant resources. However, they did not care for the poor and needy. They committed and multiplied their abominations before YHWH (50). Sodom's abominations seem to refer to the evil deeds of Gen. 18:16-19:38. YHWH said he had removed them when he saw them(50). He destroyed her. Samaria also committed abominations. Then what about Jerusalem? YHWH said, "Yet you have not merely walked in their ways or done according to their abominations; but, as if that were too little, you acted more corruptly in all your conduct than they"(47). Samaria did not commit half of the sins of Jerusalem. Jerusalem committed more abominable sins than Samaria and Sodom did. As a result, Jerusalem made both of them appear righteous and she will be ashamed and bear disgrace(52).

b) *Sodom and Samaria being a comfort to Jerusalem (16:53-59)*

53 "Nevertheless, I will restore their captivity, the captivity of Sodom and her daughters, the captivity of Samaria and her daughters, and along with them your own captivity,
54 in order that you may bear your humiliation, and feel ashamed for all that you have done when you become a consolation to them.
55 "And your sisters, Sodom with her daughters and Samaria with her daughters, will return to their former state, and you with your daughters will also return to your former state.
56 "As the name of your sister Sodom was not heard from your lips in your day of pride,
57 before your wickedness was uncovered, so now you have become the reproach of the daughters of Edom, and of all who are around her, of the daughters of the Philistines - those surrounding you who despise you.
58 "You have borne the penalty of your lewdness and abominations," YHWH declares.
59 For thus says the Lord YHWH, "I will also do with you as you have done,

> you who have despised the oath by breaking the covenant."

Since Jerusalem made Samaria and Sodom righteous, YHWH is going to restore them from their captivity with her. Thus, Samaria and her daughters and Sodom and her daughters will also be restored to their old status and glory. On the other hand the restoration of those cities will bring unbearable humiliation and shame to Jerusalem because YHWH made no distinction between Jerusalem and those cities she despised. This treatment of YHWH became a consolation to those cities. In the previous section, the corruption and defilement of Jerusalem made Samaria and Sodom righteous, but in this section the restoration of Jerusalem became a consolation to those cities. Because of her rebellion and ardent idol worship Jerusalem lost her privileges as a chosen people and became equal with the gentiles, a lesser people even than they. The main reason for this was that Jerusalem broke her covenant with YHWH. Thus he says, "I will also do with you as you have done, you who have despised the oath by breaking the covenant"(59). The covenant was a marriage covenant made on Mount Sinai between YHWH and Israel. However, the covenant was broken by Israel playing the harlot. Therefore, YHWH is going to reward Israel according to her deeds. YHWH's basic principle of judgment is to reward according to deeds (43, 59).

(5) The Restoration of Jerusalem (16:60-63)

The concluding verses of Ezek. 16 begin with prophecy of the restoration of Jerusalem which contains YHWH's forgiveness and eternal covenant with her.

> 60 "Nevertheless, I will remember my covenant with you in the days of your youth, and I will establish an everlasting covenant with you.
> 61 "Then you will remember your ways and be ashamed when you receive your sisters, both your older and your younger; and I will give them to you as daughters, but not because of your covenant.
> 62 "Thus I will establish my covenant with you, and you shall know that I am YHWH,
> 63 in order that you may remember and be ashamed, and never open your

The Marriage Texts

mouth anymore because of your humiliation, when I have forgiven you for all that you have done," the Lord YHWH declares.

The reason for YHWH to restore Jerusalem is his remembrance of the covenant he made with Israel at Mount Sinai. Even though Israel betrayed him and broke the covenant, he did not forget it. The covenant is the basis for his restoration of Israel. YHWH's restoration is to forgive her apostasy and rebellions and establish an everlasting covenant with her. The Hebrew phrase, *hēqîm berit* (הקים ברית, "to establish a covenant") is different from *kāraṯ bᵉriṯ* (כרת ברית, "to make a covenant") in its meaning. In most cases *kāraṯ bᵉriṯ* (כרת ברית) is used for making a new covenant in the Bible (Ezek. 34:25; 37:26), but *hēqîm bᵉriṯ* (הקים ברית) is used not only for making a new covenant (Gen. 6:18; Ex. 6:4) but for maintaining a covenant already concluded (Gen. 17:19, 21; Lev. 26:9; Deut. 8:18, etc.).[31] "The covenant made in the days of youth" in verse 60 has continuity with "the everlasting covenant," and the former is the origin and motivation of the latter.

YHWH shows his faithfulness in his restoration of Israel and the establishment of an everlasting covenant with her. Through this renewed relationship the anger and wrath of YHWH will be appeased and the sins of Israel forgiven and her status restored to the same position as before her election. Thus Israel will be ashamed of her past, but she will entertain Samaria and Sodom, her sisters. Even YHWH will give them as her daughters. This means that he will give them as her satellite cities and she will be responsible for their security.

When YHWH establishes an everlasting covenant with her and gives Samaria and Sodom as her daughters, Jerusalem will be restored to the past glory. However, this presupposes the process of "forgiveness." The meaning of forgiveness here is not simply accepting the rebellious sons and adulterous wife without any reproach or punishment. It requires atonement. The Hebrew word, *ka par* (כפר), rendered here as "to forgive," is a technical cultic term meaning "to atone," "to ransom." Whatever philological meaning its ancient Semitic cognate may have, it is common and clear that it meant to shed blood and pay the costly price of life in order for anyone to be forgiven.

31. Ibid., 291.

YHWH, THE HUSBAND OF ISRAEL

What is the reason for YHWH to forgive Israel's sin and establish a covenant with her? The first answer for this is that it was to make YHWH himself known to Jerusalem, that he is YHWH. The name YHWH implies power, sovereignty, holiness, and his position as the author and controller of events. The present Jerusalem does not acknowledge him as such, but at the time of the restoration she will know that he is the controller of history and the lord of judgement. The second answer is that it was to make Jerusalem give him thanks and praise him. However, verse 63 suggests that there is something more beyond forgiveness. YHWH makes her remember her past sins and be ashamed of them. YHWH is the one who forgives the sins of his people and never remembers them (Jer. 31:34; Is. 54:4). However, even though YHWH does not remember our sins, we cannot forget our sins. We may recall and remember our past deeds and take a pattern for our future life. Whenever we recall what has happened, we may praise and glorify him for his forgiving grace and give thanks to him. YHWH does not remember our sins, but he causes us to remember our sins.

As has been observed, Ezekiel 16 portrays the YHWH-Israel relationship in terms of a husband-wife relationship. The series of events of a male and female's engagement, marriage, and divorce are used to denote the theological themes of election, covenant, sanction, and restoration in Israel's history. Before Israel was taken by YHWH as his people, she was like a girl abandoned at her birth in the open field. They were the slaves of Pharaoh in Egypt. However, YHWH delivered her from the bondage of Pharaoh and led her to Mount Sinai. He made a covenant with her on that mount. YHWH became her God and Israel became his people. He then settled his people in Canaan, the promised land flowing with milk and honey, the land he gave his people as her possession. Israel became a great and glorious nation. Unfortunately, Israel was not satisfied with YHWH. She worshipped other gods and followed gentile practices and customs. She burnt her children and made offerings to idols and was dependent on the military power of neighboring countries rather than YHWH for her national security. She rebelled against him. Therefore, YHWH brought in the nations on whom she depended and let them attack and destroy her. He caused Israel to be taken to Assyria and Babylon as captives. However, after 70 years, YHWH restored the fate of his people because of his covenant with them. As the husband-wife relationship is the most intimate, personal, covenantal and holy one, the YHWH-Israel relationship also carries the same character. Through this marriage metaphor

The Marriage Texts

Israel understood the nature and character of her relationship with YHWH. YHWH was her husband and she was his wife. This covenantal relationship will never be destroyed.

B. Ezekiel 23:1-49

Ezekiel 23 describes Israel's history in terms of the marriage metaphor and her unfaithfulness to the covenant with YHWH and his sanctions against her as was found in Ezek. 16. The former chapter is clearer than the latter in its theme and issue as well as its metaphorical comparison. Ezek. 23 is fundamentally different from Ezek. 16 in describing both southern and northern kingdoms as two sisters, Oholah and Oholibah, and as the wives of YHWH. This is closer to Jeremiah 3. Even though it emphasizes the sins and punishment of Israel, the omission of restoration is another peculiar point of Ezek. 23. The language used in this chapter is very vivid and vulgar in describing Israel's apostasy.

The author seems to intentionally choose this type of language in order to emphasize Israel's betrayal and apostasy. Ezek. 23 can be divided into 4 paragraphs.

(1) The harlotry of Oholah and Oholibah (1-4)
(2) The harlotry and punishment of Oholah (5-10)
(3) The harlotry and punishment of Oholibah (11-35)
(4) The punishment of Oholah and Oholibah (36-49)

Verses 1-4 are an introduction, and YHWH accuses his spouses, Oholah and Oholibah, of their harlotries. Verses 5-35 describe each of the harlotries of the two sisters and the following punishment. YHWH's judgment on them is recorded in verses 36-49.

(1) The Harlotry of Oholah and Oholibah (23:1-4)

This portion is the introduction of Ezek. 23. Both kingdoms of Israel are here described as two sisters born of one mother and as the wives of YHWH.

YHWH, THE HUSBAND OF ISRAEL

Ezekiel the prophet is saying that these words came to him from YHWH.

1 The word of YHWH came to me again saying,
2 "Son of man, there were two women, the daughters of one mother;
3 and they played the harlot in Egypt. They played the harlot in their youth; there their breasts were pressed, and there their virgin bosom was handled.
4 "And their names were Oholah the elder and Oholibah her sister. And they became mine, and they bore sons and daughters. And as for their names, Samaria is Oholah, and Jerusalem is Oholibah.

The common origin of the two sisters is here introduced. The name of one is Oholah representing Samaria, the other is Oholibah representing Jerusalem. These two cities are the capitals of the divided kingdoms of Israel. This, therefore, is the story of Israel as a nation. The Hebrew term Oholah means "her tent"(אהלה) and Oholibah, "my tent is in her" (אהליבה). The exact symbolic meanings of these names are not known.[32] However, it is clear that they were adulterous sisters in their youth, in the land of Egypt under the bondage of Pharaoh (3, 8). Their adulterous habits could historically be traced back to the ancient time before YHWH chose them as his people.

(2) The Harlotry and Punishment of Oholah(23:5-10)

Ezek. 23: 5-10 details Oholah's harlotry and her following punishment by YHWH. Samaria's idol worship and military dependence upon her neighbors rather than her covenantal God are described in terms of harlotry and are dealt with as such. YHWH's accusation of Oholah's sin is described in verses 5-8 and his punishment in 9-10.

5 "And Oholah played the harlot while she was mine; and she lusted after her lovers, after the Assyrians, her neighbors,

---

32. Scholars have proposed different opinions about the meaning of "tent." Some say it was a kind of marriage tent that was pitched for Absalom on the roof in order to lay with his father's concubines in the sight of all Israel (2 Sam. 16:22). Others say it was a "tent of meeting" called a tabernacle. Since the name of Oholibamah (אהליבמה, tent of high place), the wife of Esau, refers to the tent of the gods in Ugaritic literature, Oholah and Oholibah are attested to be temples of the gentile gods. Taylor, 171. Leslie C. Allen, *Ezekiel 20-48*.

6 who were clothed in purple, governors and officials, all of them desirable young men, horsemen riding on horses.
7 "And she bestowed her harlotries on them, all of whom were the choicest men of Assyria; and with all whom she lusted after, with all their idols she defiled herself.
8 "And she did not forsake her harlotries from the time in Egypt; for in her youth men had lain with her, and the handled her virgin bosom and poured out their lust on her.
9 "Therefore, I gave her into the hand of her lovers, into the hand of the Assyrians, after whom she lusted.
10 "They uncovered her nakedness; they took her sons and her daughters, but they slew her with the sword. Thus she became a by-word among women, and they executed judgments on her.

According to verse 5, Oholah was a woman who belonged to YHWH. This means that she was YHWH's wife, because a husband was the *baʿal* (בעל) of his wife, her possessor. Even though Oholah made a covenant with YHWH and became his wife, she played the harlot. Her adulterous deeds can be traced back to the period of her youth before her marriage while she was in Egypt. Her defilement is outspokenly described in verse 8. She lay with the Egyptians and they caressed her virgin bosom with their hands and poured out their lust on her. The phrase "pouring out their lust" is similar to "poured out their lewdness"(16:36) in its meaning. It is a euphemistic expression for sexual intercourse. However, her habit of playing the harlot continued even after her marriage with YHWH and she loved Assyria. The Assyrians are here called "neighbors," "governors and officials," and "horsemen riding on horses." The word *qᵉrôbîm* (קרובים), translated here as "neighbors," has been understood as the derivative of *qārab* (קרב) carrying the meaning of "to be near," "to draw near." However, historically Israel, particularly the northern kingdom, had never been neighbors with the Assyrians. Since the later Hebrew *qerab* (קרב) is used with the meaning of "to war," or "to be ready for war," modern versions render it as "warriors" (קרוב).[33] The purple clothing was certain to draw the attention of women, since it was so luxurious and beautiful. The merchants of Tyre decorated the awnings of their ships with this (27:7), and the tabernacle and the priestly clothes in the Bible were to use purple (Ex. 25; Num. 4; 15:38). Gentiles used it in clothing their idols

---

33. NIV, NKJV, Zimmerli, 472., Cooke, 250.

(Jer. 10:9) and in the furnishing of the royal festival chamber (Esth. 1:6).[34] The Hebrew term, *pehā* (פחה), rendered here as "governors," is an Akkadian loan word abbreviated from *bēl piḥati* which means "ambassador," and *sagan* (סגן) is also a loan word from the Akkadian *šaknu* which means "ambassador" or "representative" (Jer. 51:23, 57; Dan. 3:2 f; 27).[35] The Assyrians are here described as "desirable young men" and "horsemen riding on horses," because they were young and energetic soldiers. The Samaritans, called here as Oholah, loved those Assyrians (5). Historically, this may refer to Jehu who prostrated himself before the king of Assyria (840 B.C.), offering him gifts while requesting military aid against the raid of Hazael of Damascus. Or it may refer to Menahem who strengthened his throne by giving Pul, the king of Assyria, a thousand talents of silver exacted from all the mighty men of wealth (2 Kgs. 15:19ff). It may also refer to Hoshea who paid tribute to Shalmaneser (2 Kgs. 17:3).[36] In this way, the Samaritans were dependent upon Assyria for their life and security by offering money and gifts to them without any regard for YHWH. Thus he compares her to a woman who played the harlot.

How does YHWH punish Oholah ? He gave her into the hand of her lovers, into the hand of the Assyrians after whom she lusted in order that they might uncover her nakedness and take her children, and finally that they might slay her with the sword. YHWH will destroy her through the hand of her lovers. He rewards her according to her deeds.

(3) The Harlotry and Punishment of Oholibah (23:11-35)

The accusations and judgments of YHWH now turn to Oholibah, the sister of Oholah. Even though Oholibah took notice of Oholah's tragic downfall brought on by playing the harlot, she disregarded this and practiced even more abominable things than her sister. She betrayed YHWH her husband. Jerusalem did not learn the lesson of Samaria's fate. In the first section (11-21), Ezekiel describes Oholibah playing the harlot with Assyria (11-13), with

---

34. Zimmerli, 484-5.
35. Zimmerli, 485, Cook, 250.
36. John B. Taylor, 172.

The Marriage Texts

Babylon (14-18) and with Egypt (19-21). The repeated and typical phrases, "yet she was more corrupt in her lust"(11), "so she increased her harlotries"(14), and "yet she multiplied her harlotries"(19), emphasize the fact that Oholibah's harlotries were more than those of her sister, Oholah. In the second section, verses 22-35 describe YHWH's judgment on a corrupted Jerusalem. This section consists of four oracles beginning with the instruction key: "Thus says YHWH God"(22, 28, 32, 35). In verses 22-30, YHWH brings in Oholibah's enemies to avenge her betrayal, and in verses 31-35 YHWH had Oholibah drink the cup of desolation, eventually letting her die. Thus, this section can be outlined as follows:

1. Oholibah, more corrupt than Oholah (11-21)
   (1) Playing the harlot with Assyria (11-13)
   (2) Playing the harlot with Babylon (14-18)
   (3) Playing the harlot with Egypt (19-21)
2. YHWH, punishing Oholibah (22-35)
   (1) Punishment through her lovers (22-35)
   (2) Punishment through the cup of desolation (31-25)

a. Oholibah, more corrupt than Oholah (23:11-21)

Oholibah was more corrupt than Oholah her sister. YHWH pointed out her corruptness, her playing the harlot with Assyria (11-13), Babylon(14-18), and Egypt (19-21). He was also concerned about the degree of her corruption. She was far worse than the usual harlots.

11 Now her sister Oholibah saw this, yet she was more corrupt in her lust than she, and her harlotries were more than the harlotries of her sister.
12 "She lusted after the Assyrians, governors and officials, the ones near, magnificently dressed, horsemen riding on horses, all of them desirable young men.
13 "And I saw that she had defiled herself; they both took the sam way.
14 "So she increased her harlotries. And she saw men portrayed on the wall, images of the Chaldeans portrayed with vermilion,
15 girded with belts on their loins, with flowing turbans on their heads, all of them looking like officers, like the Babylonians of Chaldea, the land of their birth.

16 "And when she saw them she lusted after them and sent messengers to them in Chaldea.
17 "And the Babylonians came to her to the bed of love, and they defiled her with their harlotry. And when she had been defiled by them, she became disgusted with them.
18 "And she uncovered her harlotries and uncovered her nakedness; then I became disgusted with her, as I had become disgusted with her sister.
19 "Yet she multiplied her harlotries, remembering the days of her youth, when she played the harlot in the land of Egypt.
20 "And she lusted after their paramours, whose flesh is like the flesh of donkeys and whose issue is like the issue of horses.
21 "Thus you longed for the lewdness of your youth, when the Egyptians handled your bosom because of the breasts of your youth.

In this section Oholibah's corruption and harlotry are described, which are more abominable than those of Oholah. This metaphor obviously refers to Judah's betrayal of her Lord, YHWH, and to her corruption of playing the harlot.

First of all, her actions were deliberate and willful. Oholibah saw the tragic fate of Oholah's harlotry. Nevertheless, she continued to play the harlot. She knew what the results would be of her rebellion and apostasy. But she did not stop and repent. She deliberately played the harlot. She disregarded the judgment of YHWH. She was haughty and arrogant. Secondly, the number of Oholibah's lovers was greater than that of her sister's. Oholah had only one lover, Assyria. However, Oholibah played the harlot not only with Assyria, but with Babylon and even with Egypt. She gave her love to anyone indiscriminately. Thirdly, her manner of playing the harlot was more abominable. The Assyrians are described as the ones "who [were] clothed in purple, governors and officials, all of them desirable young men, horsemen riding on horses"(6, 12). Oholibah played the harlot with these Assyrians as her sister did. However, she was not satisfied with the Assyrians. She saw men portrayed on a wall, figures of Chaldeans portrayed in red, with belts round their waists and flowing turbans on their heads; all of them looked like Babylonian chariot officers, natives of Chaldea. As soon as she saw them, she lusted after them and sent messengers to them in Chaldea. Then Babylon came to her, to the bed of love, and in their lust they defiled her. After she had been defiled by them, she turned away from them in disgust. In this way, Oholibah called anyone to her that could satisfy her sexual desire. Therefore, YHWH turned away from her in disgust, just as he had turned away from her sister, Oholah. However, she did not stop there. She recalled the days of her youth, when she was a prostitute in Egypt. There she lusted after her lovers, whose genitals were like those of donkeys and whose emission was like that of horses (20).

Oholibah's lewdness is satirized and compared to Judah's history which had been characterized by dependence upon the military powers of foreign nations. The historicity of Judah's relationship with Assyria can be traced back to the time of Ahaz, when the Syro-Ephramite coalition invaded Judah. Ahaz of Judah took the silver and gold found in the temple of YHWH and in the treasuries of the royal palace and sent it as a gift to Tiglath-pileser, king of Assyria, in order to gain his military aid (2 Kgs. 16:8). The prophet Isaiah strongly advised Ahaz to trust YHWH, but he did not hear him (Isa. 7:7-9).

The correct historical background of the relationship between Judah and Babylon needs to be pointed out. Babylon was the successor to Assyrian rule in Mesopotamia. During the reign of Hezekiah, Merodach-Baladan, the son of Baladan king of Babylon, sent envoys to Hezekiah with letters and a gift, because he had heard of Hezekiah's illness. Hezekiah received the messengers and showed them all that was in his storehouse. He exposed the heart of his kingdom to the Babylonians. Isaiah, the prophet, checked this and rebuked the king's imprudence and prophesied the coming of Babylon to carry them off in the near future (2 Kgs. 20:12-20). This prophecy was actually realized at the end of the nation. Babylon invaded Judah, and Judah became the vassal of Babylon. Jehoiakim became the vassal of Nebuchadnezzar for three years. His son Jehoiachin succeeded him as king. Nebuchadnezzar came to Jerusalem and laid siege to it. The king of Judah surrendered and was taken to Babylon as a prisoner. The king of Babylon took away all the treasures, the gold articles from the temple and royal palace. He carried into exile almost all of the inhabitants of Jerusalem, approximately ten thousand people. Only the poorest people of the land were left. Nebuchadnezzar made Mattaniah, Johoiachin's uncle, king in his place and changed his name to Zedekiah.

However, Zedekiah, the vassal of Babylon, asked for military help from Neco, the Egyptian king, in order to gain independence from Nebuchadnezzar. Unfortunately this plan failed. Nebuchadnezzar defeated Neco at Carchmish and marched against Jerusalem with his whole army. He set fire to the temple of YHWH, the royal palace and all the house of Jerusalem. Nebuchadnezzar killed the sons of Zedekiah in front of him, then put out his eyes, bound him with bronze shackles and took him to Babylon.

Thus, Oholibah's relationship with Egypt is clear. The kings of Judah tried to get military aid from Egypt in order to be independent from Babylon. However, Egypt was not strong enough to save Judah from the hand of Babylon (Jer. 2:18; 37:7; Lam. 4:17).YHWH regarded it as rebellion and adultery when his people were dependent upon foreign nations and powers other than him for their national security.

b. *YHWH, punishing Oholibah (23:22-35)*

This section consists of four oracles beginning with the formula: "Thus says YHWH God"(כה אמר אדני יהוה, 22, 28, 32, 35). These oracles describe YHWH's judgment on Jerusalem in the form of an allegory.

a) Judgment through her lovers (23:22-27)

22 "Therefore, O Oholibah, thus says YHWH GOD, 'Behold I will arouse your lovers against you, from whom you were alienated, and I will bring them against you from every side:
23 the Babylonians and all the Chaldeans, Pekod and Shoa and Koa, and all the Assyrians with them; desirable young men, governors and officials all of them, officers and men of renown, all of them riding on horses.
24 'And they will come against you with weapons, chariots, and wagons, and with a company of peoples. They will set themselves against you on every side with buckler and shield and helmet; and I shall commit the judgment to them, and they will judge you according to their customs.
25 'And I will set my jealousy against you, that they may deal with you in wrath. They will remove your nose and your ears; and your survivors will fall by the sword. They will take your sons and your daughters; and your survivors will be consumed by the fire.
26 'They will also strip you of your clothes and take away your beautiful jewels.
27 'Thus I shall make your lewdness and your harlotry brought from the land

of Egypt to cease from you, so that you will not lift up your eyes to them or remember Egypt anymore.'

YHWH's judgment on Oholibah was to stimulate the heart of those who were betrayed by her to burn with jealousy and to incur their hatred so that they would attack and take vengeance on her. The foreign lovers YHWH summoned together to attack and surround her were the Babylonians and all the Chaldeans, the men of Pekod and Shoa and Koa, and all the Assyrians with them. The men of Pekod and Shoa and Koa are normally identified, though not without some uncertainty, with *Puqûdu, Sutû* and *Qutû* Aramaean tribes to the east of the River Tigris which are known from a number of Assyrian and Babylonian inscriptions.[37] They were handsome young men, all of them governors and commanders, chariot officers and men of high rank, all mounted on horses. YHWH will call them in against her and they will surround her with weapons, chariots and wagons, with large and small shields and helmets. YHWH will hand her over to them for punishment and they will punish her according to their standard (24). When he pours out his jealous anger against her, they will deal with her in fury. They will cut off her nose and ears. They will take away her sons and daughters and they will burn her with fire. They will also strip her of her clothes and take her fine jewelry (25). Thus, he will stop her from playing the harlot, an activity which she began in Egypt. She will not look on these abominable things with longing or remember Egypt any more.

Even though those foreign lovers would inflict a cruel punishment upon Oholibah as described in verse 25, it was ultimately YHWH who was behind the punishment and would execute the judgment. The foreign powers were nothing but the instruments of YHWH's punishment upon Jerusalem.

b) Punishment through the cup of desolation (23:28-35)

28 "For thus says YHWH GOD, 'Behold, I will give you into the hand of those whom you hate, into the hand of those from whom you were alienated.

---

37. The men of Pekod and Shoa and Koa are normally identified as *Puqûdu, Sutû* and *Qutu*, Aramaean tribes to the east of the River Tigris which are known from a number of Assyrian and Babylonian inscriptions. Taylor,174.

29 'And they will deal with you in hatred, take all your property, and leave you naked and bare. And the nakedness of your harlotries shall be uncovered, both your lewdness and your harlotries.
30 'These things will be done to you because you have played the harlot with the nations, because you have defiled yourself with their idols.
31 'You have walked in the way of your sister; therefore I will give her cup into your hand.'
32 "Thus says YHWH GOD, 'You will drink your sister's cup, which is deep and wide. You will be laughed at and held in derision; It contains much.
33 'You will be filled with drunkenness and sorrow, The cup of horror and desolation, The cup of your sister Samaria.
34 'And you will drink it and drain it. Then you will gnaw its fragments and tear your breasts; for I have spoken,' declares YHWH GOD.
35 'Therefore, thus says YHWH GOD, 'Because you have forgotten me and cast me behind your back, bear now the punishment of your lewdness and your harlotries.'"

The other way YHWH would mete out punishment on Oholibah was to hand her over to those whom she hated so that they might deal with her in hatred and expose her nakedness and prostitution. The principle of reciprocity is maintained (31). Furthermore, YHWH was going to give her sister's cup into her hand, the cup of desolation. This cup is here designated as "her cup," "your sister's cup," "the cup of your sister Samaria," "the cup of horror and desolation." It is a metaphoric description of fate and death. The cup is the vessel flowing with YHWH's anger and wrath (Ps. 75:8; Isa. 51:17, 22; Jer. 25:15-29; 49:12; Lam. 4:21; Obad. 16; Hab. 2:16; Matt. 20:22; 26:39; Rev. 14:10). When Oholibah drank it, she would be out of herself. She would break it and tear apart her breasts with the broken pieces and eventually die in her pain. YHWH caused her to pay the price of her rebellion and adultery in this way.

(4) The Judgment on Oholibah and Oholah (23:36-49)

The writer of this metaphor dealt with the harlotries of Oholibah and Oholah in verses 1-4 and YHWH's judgments on each of the sisters in verses 5-10 and 11-35. Now in the final section Ezekiel recapitulates and expands the judgments that have gone before. This section is composed of the accusations

The Marriage Texts

against religious sins (36-39), political sins (40-45) and the ensuing judgment of YHWH on those who played the harlot (46-49).

36 Moreover, YHWH said to me, "Son of man, will you judge Oholah and Oholibah? Then declare to them their abominations.
37 "For they have committed adultery, and blood is on their hands. Thus they have committed adultery with their idols and even caused their sons, whom they bore to me, to pass through the fire to them as food.
38 "Again, they have done this to me: they have defiled my sanctuary on the same day and have profaned my sabbaths.
39 "For when they had slaughtered their children for their idols, they entered my sanctuary on the same day to profane it; and lo, thus they did within my house.
40 "Furthermore, they have even sent for men who come from afar, to whom a messenger was sent; and lo, they came - for whom you bathed, painted your eyes, and decorated yourselves with ornaments;
41 and you sat on a splendid couch with a table arranged before it, on which you had set my incense and my oil.
42 "And the sound of a carefree multitude was with her; and drunkards were brought from the wilderness with men of the common sort. And they put bracelets on the hands of the women and beautiful crowns on their heads.
43 "Then I said concerning her who was worn out by adulteries, 'Will they now commit adultery with her when she is thus?'
44 "But they went in to her as they would go in to a harlot. Thus they went in to Oholah and to Oholibah, the lewd women.
45 "But they, righteous men, will judge them with the judgment of adulteresses, and with the judgment of women who shed blood, because they are adulteresses and blood is on their hands.
46 "For thus says YHWH GOD, 'Bring up a company against them, and give them over to terror and plunder.
47 'And the company will stone them with stones and cut them down with their swords; they will slay their sons and their daughters and burn their houses with fire.
48 'Thus I shall make lewdness cease from the land, that all women may be admonished and not commit lewdness as you have done.
49 'And your lewdness will be requited upon you, and you will bear the penalty of worshiping your idols; thus you will know that I am YHWH GOD.'"

Ezekiel again recounts the harlotries of Oholah and Oholibah in verses 36-39. Most of them are Israel's religious sins. They were not only worshiping idols and offering child-sacrifices, but also playing the harlot on the sabbath (38) and defiling YHWH's sanctuary. The temple and sabbath had to be kept holy and respected according to the laws. However, they despised YHWH.

Ezekiel accuses Israel using a metaphor that compares their military dependency upon foreign nations to harlotry in verses 40-45. Oholibah and Oholah invited the foreigners, and when they arrived, both sisters bathed themselves for them, painted their eyes, and put on their jewelry. The women entertained them by spreading the table of YHWH for them. They used his incense and oil for the foreigners. The foreigners in return put bracelets on the arms of the women and beautiful crowns on their heads (42). Soon the foreigners used the sisters as their prostitutes. As men sleep with a prostitute, so they slept with these lewd women, Oholibah and Oholah (43). Thus YHWH is going to punish them as he does a woman who commits adultery and sheds blood, because they are adulterous and blood is on their hands (45).

In verses 46-49, YHWH proclaims his judgment on the sisters. He brings a mob against them and gives them over to terror and plunder. Then the mob will stone them and cut them down with their swords. They will kill their sons and daughters and burn down their houses. Thus, he is going to put an end to lewdness in the land. All the women in the land will take warning from this and will not imitate their crime. Death by stoning and destruction of their property with fire were the common penalties for all adulteresses and shedders of blood in those days (cf. Lev. 20:10; Deut. 21:21). Ezekiel portrays the coming destruction of Jerusalem in terms of the punishment of his adulterous wives. They will suffer the penalty for their lewdness and bear the consequences of their sins of idolatry. After this they will know that he is the sovereign YHWH.

5. OTHER TEXTS

In addition to the texts that have been surveyed thus far, there are many other passages and phrases, particularly in the prophetical books that portray YHWH and Israel as a husband and wife. However, those do not constitute the story of the engagement, marriage, divorce, and remarriage of one couple as we have seen in Hosea, Jeremiah, and Ezekiel. However, they do compare

The Marriage Texts

the idol worship and religious degradation of Israel to a harlot or a woman who has committed adultery. In this case the prophets accuse Israel simply of being a "harlot," or "adulterer." This presupposes the YHWH-Israel relationship to be that of a married couple, and the people of Israel seemed to be accustomed to the metaphor of a marriage relationship.

In Isa. 50:1, YHWH asked Israel, who had been exiled to Babylon, "Where is the certificate of divorce by which I have sent your mother away?" As has been observed in Jer. 3:8, YHWH regarded his destruction of Jerusalem and the captivity of Israel in Babylon as a divorce between him and Israel. Now he is going to withdraw the divorce and take her again as his wife. Thus he requests that the bill of divorce be brought.

In Isa. 54:1-8, YHWH introduces himself as "Your husband is your maker, whose name is YHWH of hosts"(5). He thus calls the captive Israel "a wife forsaken and grieved in spirit," and "a wife of one's youth when she is rejected"(6). Now he plans to return to his wife because he has not rejected her permanently. He promises to deliver her.

> "For a brief moment I forsook you,
> But with great compassion I will gather you.
> In an outburst of anger
> I hid my face from you for a moment:
> But with everlasting lovingkindness,
> I will have compassion on you." (Isa. 54:7-8)

It can also be observed here that YHWH is described as the husband of Israel, and the fall and restoration of Israel as a divorce and remarriage. He forsook Israel and hid his face from her, but it was for a brief moment. He did not abandon her permanently. He will restore her with everlasting kindness. According to this promise, the period of the Babylonian exile is not to be understood as his permanent rejection of his people.

Isa. 57:1-10 describes YHWH's rebuke of Israel's apostasy, particularly the worship of Baal on the high places and the abominable practice of child sacrifice to Molech. He calls Israel the "offspring of an adulterer and a prostitute"(3) and the ones "who inflame themselves among the oak and under every luxuriant tree"(5). YHWH said again in verse 8,

YHWH, THE HUSBAND OF ISRAEL

> Indeed, far removed from me,
> You have uncovered yourself
> And have gone up and made your bed wide,
> And you have agreement for yourselves with them,
> You have loved their bed,
> You have looked on their manhood. (Is. 57:8)

The apostasy of Israel is described in terms of the metaphor of a married woman who has committed adultery and is playing the harlot.

Is. 62:1-5 gives a word about the restoration of Zion. Since Zion refers to Israel, this paragraph also describes the marriage relationship between YHWH and Israel. Zion will no longer be called "forsaken" or "desolate," but "$hepsî$-bah"(חפצי־בה) or "$b^{e\text{c}}ulâ$" (בעולה). The word "forsaken" refers to a woman who has been abandoned by her husband and "desolate" refers to a woman of barrenness. Whereas the word "$hepsî$-bah "(חפצי־בה) means "My delight is in her," it refers to the case of restoring the love of a husband. Since "$b^{e\text{c}}ulâ$ " (בעולה) means "married," it carries the opposite meaning of "forsaken," or "desolate." Zion is personified and described here as a divorced, as well as a remarried, woman. This metaphor presupposes the marriage relationship between YHWH and Israel.

In summary, the marriage texts are found mainly in Hosea, Jeremiah and Ezekiel, and partly in the context of the restoration in Isaiah. Perhaps the theological concern about the YHWH-Israel relationship after the fall of both kingdoms seems to create the metaphor of marriage. The marriage metaphor is first found in Hosea, but word studies as well as studies of the marriage formula and covenant formula show that its origin can be traced back to ancient Israel. The marriage metaphor in Hosea is more refined in the book of Jeremiah. Jeremiah's comparison of the Sinai covenant to a marriage and of the new covenant to remarriage are significant to the understanding and interpretation of the covenant between YHWH and Israel. Jeremiah's theological insights made the marriage metaphor as an organic live metaphor possible.

The marriage metaphors in the book of Ezekiel are the expanded and complemented versions of Hosea and Jeremiah. Each of the metaphors constitutes a perfect story. Though it follows the plot of Hosea, the concept of adultery is expanded to the political and military dependence upon foreign nations. The story of two sisters, Oholah and Oholibah, is obviously a metaphor that is expanded from Jer. 3. Because of this, we may say that the marriage metaphors in Ezekiel are more beautiful, abundant, and adequate in the sense of theology and literature.

The marriage metaphors were developed with the history of Israel. Israel created them in order to understand God better and to have a more holy and personal relationship with him. Their major religious concern was their relationship with YHWH. Their intimate and exclusive relationship with YHWH was recognized from an early date. They interpreted the major events in their national history, such as election, covenant, rejection and restoration, in terms of a husband-wife relationship. The series of historical events were compared to a couple's engagement, marriage, divorce, and remarriage.

CHAPTER VI

Christ and the Church as a Husband and Wife

The marriage metaphor in the Old Testament describing the relationship between YHWH and Israel in terms of a husband and wife is also found in the New Testament. Jesus and his disciples, particularly Jesus and his church, are portrayed as a husband and wife. A survey of the NT texts and an examination of their continuity with the OT is appropriate at this point. Furthermore, the task is to understand how the NT writers utilized and developed this theme. One thing to be noted here is that marriage texts in the NT are rarely found against our expectation. Mainly in the Johannine literature and Pauline epistles are Jesus and the church described as bridegroom and bride.

1. THE JOHANNINE LITERATURE
(Jn. 2:1-12; 3:22-30; Rev. 19:6-9)

The public ministry of Jesus began at the wedding feast in Cana of Galilee. His first sign as the Messiah was to make wine from water when the supply of wine was depleted. Why did Jesus show this as his first miracle at a wedding feast? The answer is not clearly given in the text. However, this implies many aspects of his identity and his relationship with the people.

In the ancient Near East, the bridegroom was to make the marriage feast for his friends and families. If not, the marriage was not publicly recognized and had no legal force. Even though a man and a girl lived together for a long period of time, without writing the bill of marriage and offering the banquet to the inhabitants of the village, the couple was not recognized as a legal husband and wife. There are examples of this in the code of Hammurabi and the laws of Eshnunna. According to these laws, if a man took a girl and lived for more than one year without the permission of their parents, without writing the certificate of marriage, and without giving a marriage feast, the couple was not legally married and could not be protected by the society and state.[1] Of course, the marriage feast was followed by a marriage contract.

In the story of the first miracle of Jesus, the master of the banquet tasted the quality wine and said to the bridegroom, "Every man serves good wine first, and when men have drunk freely, then that which is poorer ; you have kept the good wine until now"(Jn. 2:10). It can be seen here that the groom had the responsibility to provide wine to the wedding guests. However, Jesus was the real supplier of the wine in this wedding feast. This implies that Jesus is the bridegroom. When the mother of Jesus informed them that they had no more wine, Jesus seemed to have perceived that his mother was not simply reporting to him that they had no wine, but that she was asking him to do something which implied more than what she said. Thus he said to her, "What do I have to do with you? My hour has not yet come"(Jn. 2:4). It is not easy to understand the correct meaning of this dialogue between the mother and her son. Jesus is very much conscious of his time. He seems to work according to his schedule. But his hour had not come yet. However, in Revelation we can see again the scene of a wedding in which Jesus is involved. John describes the scene of the consummation as the marriage of Jesus with the believers.

> 6   And I heard, as it were, the voice of a great multitude and as the sound of many waters and as the sound of mighty peals of thunder, saying, "Hallelujah! For the Lord our God, the Almighty, reigns.
> 7   "Let us rejoice and be glad and give the glory to him , for the marriage of the Lamb has come and his bride has made herself ready."
> 8   And it was given to her to clothe herself in fine linen, bright and clean;

---

1. Reuben Yaron, *The Laws of Eshnuna* (Jerusalem-Leiden: The Magnes Press, E. J. Brill, 1969), 172-222. Samuel Greengus, "The Old Babylonian Marriage Contract," *JAOS* 89.3 (1969): 505. The Code of Hammurabi, #128, 129. The Laws of Eshnunna, #27-28.

for the fine linen is the righteous acts of the saints.
9 And he said to me, "Write, 'Blessed are those who are invited to the marriage supper of the Lamb.'" And he said to me, "These are true words of God."

When the Lord our God, the Almighty reigns, the marriage of the Lamb will come. In the Johannine literature, "the Lamb," or "the Lamb of God" is a special designation for Jesus (ὁ ἀμνος, 1:29, 36; το; ἀρνῖον, Rev. 5:7, 9; 6: 11). Thus, the bridegroom is Jesus, the Lamb of God. His bride is clothed in fine linen. And the "fine linen" is said to refer to the righteous acts of the saints. Thus, the saints can easily be understood to be the bride of Jesus. John is picturing the believer's perfect union with Christ on the day of consummation through a marriage metaphor. When Mary the mother of Jesus proposed that he assume the role of a bridegroom by providing wine at the wedding feast in Cana, he answered, "My hour has not yet come"(Jn. 2:4). But in the book of Revelation, "the marriage of the Lamb has come and His bride has made herself ready"(Rev. 19:7). From this we can find that John presented Jesus as a bridegroom in the first miracle of his public ministry, and concluded his works with the marriage of Jesus with the saints at the establishment and reigning of his kingdom over the nations.

Between the first miracle of Jesus at Cana and the marriage of the Lamb, John the Baptist called himself "the friend of the bridegroom"(Jn. 3:28-29). He said to his disciples who heard that Jesus was baptizing others and that the people were coming to him:

> You yourselves bear me witness, that I said, "I am not the Christ, but I have been sent before him. He who has the bride is the bridegroom; but the friend of the bridegroom, who stands and hears him, rejoices greatly because of the bridegroom's voice. And so this joy of mine has been made full."(Jn 3:28-29)

Here, bride, bridegroom, and the friend of bridegroom are mentioned. Of course, the bridegroom refers to Jesus, the friend of bridegroom to John the Baptist himself, and the bride to those who come to be baptized. The friend of the bridegroom is in charge of the wedding feast. The role of the friend was very important for the groom, because legal and social recognition of the marriage was acquired through the feast. Thus, one of the most intimate friends took this role of the headwaiter. John the Baptist understood Jesus' relationship with his disciples in view of the YHWH-Israel relationship in the Old Testament, that is, husband and wife. For John the Baptist, Jesus was the one who was described as the husband of Israel in the OT. He was to witness Jesus as the bridegroom and the disciples as his bride.

2. THE SYNOPTIC GOSPELS (Mk. 2:19-20; Matt. 9:15; Lk. 5:34)

There are a few passages where Jesus alluded to himself as the bridegroom when speaking to his followers in the gospels. When the disciples of John and the Pharisees came to him and asked the reason why his disciples did not fast, he answered, "While the bridegroom is with them, the attendants of the bridegroom do not fast, do they? So long as they have the bridegroom with them they cannot fast. But the days will come when the bridegroom is taken away from them, and then they will fast in that day" (Mk. 2:19-20; Matt. 9:15; Lk. 5:34). Jesus did not explicitly say who the bridegroom was, but it is clearly implied that the bridegroom refers to himself and his disciples to the attendants of the bridegroom.[2] This answer of Jesus provides a new perspective on his earthly ministry. The period of his earthly ministry is viewed as a honeymoon period between him and his followers.[3] This seems to conflict with the book of Revelation, since it describes the union of the saints with Christ at his return as a marriage between the lamb and the saints clothed with fine linen. However, it is to be noted that the relationship between Christ and the saints is established from his earthly ministry and it came to its completion at his Consummation. According to Jesus, the day will come when the bridegroom is taken away and his disciples will fast. Jesus will die on the cross and will be taken into heaven. During the time of his

---

2. John Nolland, *Luke 1-9:20* (WBC 35A; Dallas: Word, 1989), 247-48. J. J. Jeremias, (νύμφη, νυμφίος) *TDNT*, 1099-1106. "the attendants of bridegroom"(οἱ υἱοὶ τοῦ νυμφῶνος) literally means "the sons of bridal chamber," As a Hebraism, it refers to the wedding guest who is most intimate with the bridegroom. Bauer, *A Greek English Lexicon*, 547. Norval Geldenhuys, *Commentary on the Gospel of Luke* (NICNT; Grand Rapids: Eerdmans, 1951), 197.

3. J. J. Jeremias, *TDNT*, 1105.

Christ and the Church

absence on earth, it will be the time for the saints to fast. But when he returns on the last day, the saints will have perfect union with Christ. Therefore, the saints are waiting for the day of his coming just as the ten virgins waited to welcome the bridegroom with a lamp at midnight (Matt. 25:1-13).

3. THE PAULINE EPISTLES (2 Cor. 11:1-3; Eph. 5:21-33)

Among the Pauline epistles, 2 Cor. 11:1-3 and Eph. 5:22-33 are the typical texts in which Jesus and his church are compared to a bride and bridegroom.

(1) 2 Cor. 11:1-3

As Paul compares Jesus to a bridegroom and the saints to a bride, he poses himself as a mediator who matches the couple.

1 I wish that you would bear with me in a little foolishness; but indeed you are bearing with me.
2 For I am jealous for you with a godly jealousy; for I betrothed you to one husband, that to Christ I might present you as a pure virgin.
3 But I am afraid, lest as the serpent deceived Eve by his craftiness, your minds should be led astray from the simplicity and purity of devotion to Christ.

What the apostle Paul wanted from the saints of the Corinthian church was to present them to Christ as a bride. Accordingly, he compares Christ to a bridegroom, the Corinthian saints to a bride, and he thinks of himself as the matchmaker who binds the couple together. As Moses played the role of mediator between YHWH and Israel on Mount Sinai and John the Baptist played the role of the friend of the bridegroom in the metaphor of marriage between Jesus and his disciples (Jn. 3:22-30), Paul also claims this role between Christ and the Corinthians.[4] Paul's self-recognition of his role as a matchmaker can be traced back to the Sinai covenant which is portrayed as a wedding between YHWH and Israel. Particularly, the pairs of comparisons, YHWH and Jesus as bridegrooms, and Israel and the saints of the Corinthian church as brides, are noteworthy. Paul, here, identifies Jesus of the New Testament with YHWH of the OT.⁵ He calls the church "Israel of God" (ἡ Ἰσραὴλ τοῦ Θεοῦ) in several texts (Gal.3:7ff., 29; 6:16; Rom. 2:29; 4:9 ff.; Phil. 3:3). Thus, the church is the new Israel and the bride of Jesus.

Paul says that the required virtue for a bride is "the simplicity and purity of devotion to Christ," and he worries about their minds being led astray as Eve was deceived by the craftiness of the serpent. He also mentions that he is going to present "a pure virgin" to "one husband," "to Christ." He obviously emphasizes the purity and faithfulness between the couple by mentioning "one husband" and "a virgin."⁶ There cannot be two husbands for a pure bride. The godly jealousy may refer to YHWH's love for Israel in the wilderness (Ex. 20:5). As such, Paul was jealous to match both YHWH and the Corinthians.

As has been observed, Paul understands the inter-relationship of the three parties involved: Christ, the Corinthians and himself in terms of the bridegroom, bride, and matchmaker. He finds his special role in the history of redemption and recognizes the relationship between Jesus and the believers as a continuous one between YHWH and Israel in the OT.

(2) Ephesians 5:21-33

The Apostle Paul compares the relationship between Jesus and his church with that between a husband and wife in Eph. 5:21-33.

21 And be subject to one another in the fear of Christ.
22 Wives, be subject to your own husbands, as to the Lord.
23 For the husband is the head of the wife, as Christ also is the head of the church, he himself being the savior of the body.
24 But as the church is subject to Christ, so also the wives ought to be to their

---

4. Raymond D. Brown, *The Gospel According to John I-XII* (AB: Garden City: Doubleday & Company, 1985), 152.

5. Philip E. Hugh, *Commentary on the Second Epistle to the Corinthians* (NICNT; Grand Rapids: Eerdmans, 1962), 379.

6. Ralph P. Martin, *2 Corinthians* (WBC 40; Waco: Word Books, 1986), 332.

husbands in everything.
25 Husbands, love your wives, just as Christ also loved the church and gave himself up for her;
26 that he might sanctify her, having cleansed her by the washing of water with the word,
27 that he might present to himself the church in all her glory, having no spot or wrinkle or any such thing; but that she should be holy and blameless.
28 So husbands ought also to love their own wives as their own bodies. He who loves his own wife loves himself;
29 for no one ever hated his own flesh, but nourishes and cherishes it, just as Christ also does the church,
30 because we are members of his body.
31 For this cause a man shall leave his father and mother, and shall cleave to his wife; and the two shall become one flesh.
32 This mystery is great; but I am speaking with reference to Christ and the church.
33 Nevertheless let each individual among you also love his own wife even as himself; and let the wife see to it that she respect her husband.

Eph. 5:21-33 can be treated as one unit. Verse 21 concludes the exhortation to be filled with the Holy Spirit that was given in verses 18-20 and introduces a new theme, "to submit," developed in the following paragraph. Verses 21 and 33 constitute an inclusion from the perspective of meaning. Thus we can safely say that the verse 21 has a double function.[7] Paul compares the relationship between the husband and wife to the one between Jesus and the church, and exhorts the couples to respect each other and submit to one another. Paul points out the three parallel points between Jesus-church and the husband-wife.

First of all, the headship is one of the significant parallel points. As the husband is the head of his wife, Christ is also the head of his church. Paul taught that the church is the body of Christ (Eph. 1:22-23). Likewise a man and woman become one flesh through marriage (Gen. 2:24; Matt. 19:5; Mk 10:7; 1Cor. 6:16) and the husband is the head of the body. Here, the head may mean a higher authority and leadership, or the person ultimately responsible in the presence of God. Therefore, a wife must obey her husband.

The second parallel point is love. As Christ loves his church, so a husband

7. Andrew T. Lincoln, *Ephesians* (WBC 42; Dallas: Word Books, 1990), 352.

also loves his wife. How should a husband love his wife? Christ was the example. He loved his church and gave his body to her. The purpose of Christ's giving himself to his church was to sanctify her and to establish her in glory (26, 27). The holy and glorious church is the one cleansed by the washing of water with the word, having no spot or wrinkle. The church of Christ is essentially pure and glorious. Since Christ gave himself by dying on the cross and rising from the dead, his church became holy and blameless and glorious. Christ loved his church and he gave even his body to her. Likewise, a husband should love his wife. He should love his wife as his body. To love his wife is to love himself.

The third point is that the union of a husband and wife is parallel to the union of Christ and the church. As Gen. 2:24 indicates, the husband and wife became one flesh by marriage (Eph. 5:31), so Christ and his church constitute one body (30). The head of the body is Christ and its members are the believers, his church. As Christ and his church are made an inseparable organic body, so the husband and wife became an inseparable organic body.

Accordingly the headship of the husband, the love of a husband for his wife, and the inseparable union between the marriage partners are the parallel points that are also found between Christ and the church. As M. Barth has pointed out, Paul must have taken up the Old Testament imagery of a husband-wife relationship and developed it to a deeper level by means of the Christian's relationship to his Savior.[8] According to this parallelism, the Christians of the New Testament replaced the Old Testament people of Israel, and Christ replaced YHWH. Through this, Paul proclaims the deity of Christ and the church's role as the new Israel.

---

8. Markus Barth, *Ephesians*, 2 vols. (AB; Garden City: Doubleday, 1974), 2:693. See also Francis Foulkes, *The Epistle of Paul to the Ephesians* (TNTC; Grand Rapids: Eerdmans, 1963), 156.

Conclusion

The relationship between YHWH and Israel, his people, is one of the central themes of the Bible that can be explained with unity and consistency. YHWH chose Israel as his people from among many nations when they were the slaves of Pharaoh in Egypt. He made a covenant with them and entered into a legal relationship. He gave them the land of Canaan and settled them there in order that they may keep his laws and statues as his people. Through Israel YHWH prepared the restoration and salvation of the world which is under his wrath. However, Israel deserted the will of YHWH and they worshipped other gods. The nation of Israel divided into southern and northern kingdoms, and did all the evils and abominable things that YHWH hated. Thus, they lost the quality of being the chosen people. As a punishment for breaking their covenant, YHWH destroyed the northern kingdom by the hand of Assyria and the southern kingdom by Babylon. However, YHWH brought them back to their own land in order to restore them. Furthermore, he sent his promised messiah to them.

As we surveyed the history of Israel, the Bible reveals the history of the relationship between YHWH and his people, Israel. Thus, this relationship is a key to understanding and interpreting the Bible and the history in the Bible. The relationship between YHWH and Israel progresses in stages. It began with election and developed into a covenant, sin and punishment, and to restoration. These stages are not only the basic elements for the development of the YHWH-Israel relationship, but they also can be an independent theme in the Bible. However, these elements are organically related to each other, and none of them can be disregarded. As it were, the covenant cannot be explained without election, and rejection and restoration without the covenant.

The biblical writers sought the most proper and concrete way to express the relationship between YHWH and Israel, using the metaphor of a husband and wife, and employed it to describe the theological relationship that existed between them. Therefore, the marriage metaphor does not simply express the covenantal relationship. It covers the whole process of a couple's engagement, marriage, divorce and remarriage, and then it is compared to the history of Israel. This metaphor was made possible through the personification of Israel. Thus, the metaphor of marriage is theological. The relationship between YHWH and Israel, one of the major themes of the Bible, is described and portrayed through the marriage metaphor.

Until now, the theme of "election" or "covenant" has been dealt with independently as a main theme of the Bible without regard to other ones. Even "election" has been regarded as the same concept as "covenant" from time to time. However, our observations have shown that election is clearly distinguished from the covenant as an engagement is from marriage, but they are organically united with each other and one naturally follows the other. The covenant gave legal force to the election. For a young couple, an engagement alone was not enough for them to be regarded as a married couple. Without a wedding ceremony, even though they may cohabit and have children and behave like a married couple for a lengthy period of time, they are not legally or socially acknowledged as a married couple.

The Bible compares election to an engagement and the covenant to marriage. YHWH made a covenant with Israel and he took Israel as his people forever and became their God. Before he made this covenant, he could not punish them even though they opposed him and did not show fear or respect for him. However, after making the covenant and the laws were given, YHWH treated Israel according to the law. They were bound by law. Thus, election comes before the covenant and is the beginning of YHWH's sovereign relationship with Israel. The election derives legal force from the covenant and the relationship entails responsibility and obligation.

Most scholars have found the origin and form of the biblical covenant in the international political treaties of the ancient Near East, particularly of the Hittites. However, the background of the biblical covenant should not be sought only from this, but rather from the early custom of marriage. As we have observed, the formulae of both covenant and rejection were borrowed from the formulae of marriage and divorce and their character and essence are

Conclusion

very similar to those of marriage.[1] Accordingly, it should not be overlooked that the biblical concept of covenant originated from the customs of both the ancient Near Eastern treaties and marriage.

YHWH's restoration of Israel sheds new insight on the understanding of the Christian gospel. The Bible prohibits remarriage to a former wife who married another man after the initial divorce. If this is so, YHWH himself violates his law by taking Israel once again after she left him and became the possession of another. However, YHWH was not bound by his law to save and restore Israel. This comes from his *ḥeseḏ* (חסד). YHWH's love for rebellious mankind exceeds his laws. Jesus came to this world as the bridegroom of the human race which has betrayed YHWH.

---

1. Seock-Tas Sohn, "'I Will Be Your God and You Will Be My people': The Origin and Background of the Covenant Formmula." in *KI BARUCH HU* (ed. R. Chazan et al; Winona Lake: Eisenbrauns, 1999), 355-372.

Bibliography

Albright, W. F. "The High Place in Ancient Palestine" in *Volume du Congrès, Strasbourg 1956,* VT Suppl. 4. Leiden: E. J. Brill, 1957.
Allen, Leslie C. *Ezekiel 20-48,* WBC 29. Dallas: Word Books, 1990.
Andersen, F. I. and D. N. Freedman. *Hosea,* Anchor Bible. Garden City: Doubleday, 1984.
Astour, M. "The Origin of the Terms 'Canaan,' 'Phoenician,' and 'Purple,'" *JNES* 24. 1965.
Barth, Markus. *Ephesians 4-6,* Anchor Bible. Garden City: Doubleday & Co., 1974.
Bauer, Walther. *A Greek-English Lexicon of the New Testament and Other Early Christain Literature.* Chicago: Chicago University Press, 1957.
Bright, John. *Jeremiah,* Anchor Bible. Garden City:Doubleday, 1965.
_____. *A History of Israel.* Philadelphia: Westminster, 1981.
Brown, Raymond D. *The Gospel According to John I-XII,* AB. Garden City: Doubleday & Company, 1985.
Brownlee, William H. *Ezekiel 1-19,* WBC 28. Waco:Word Book,1986.
Burrows, Miller. *The Basis of Israelite Marriage.* New Haven: American Oriental Society, 1938.
Burrows, Miller. "The Ancient Oriental Background of Hebrew Levirate Marriage," *BASOR* 76. Dec., 1939.
Campbell, Edward F. Jr. *Ruth,* Anchor Bible. Garden City: Doubleday & Company, 1978.
Clement, R. E. *Exodus.* The Cambridge Bible Commentary. Cambridge: Cambridge University Press, 1972.
Cole. A. *Exodus.* Tyndale Old Testament Commentary. London: Tyndale Press, 1973.
Cooke, G. A. *Ezekiel,* The International Critical Commentary. Edinburgh: T. & T. Clark, 1972.
Cowley, A. P. *Aramaic Papyri of Fith Century B. C.* Oxford: Clarendon, 1923.

Coxe Jr., E. B. "Expedition to Egypt" *The Museum Journal*. Philadelphia: University of Pennsylvania, 1924.

Craigie, P. C. *Jeremiah 1-25*. WBC 26. Waco: Word Press,1996.

Craigie, P. C. *The Book of Deuteronomy*. The New International Commentary of the Old Testament. Grand Rapids: Eerdmans, 1976.

DeRoche, Michael. "Jeremiah 2:2-3 and Israelite Love for God during the Wilderness Wandering," *CBQ* 45, 1983.

Durham, J. L. *Exodus*. WBC. Waco: Word Books, 1987.

Eissfeldt, O. *Palastina-Jahrbuch* 27 (1931) 58-66.

Epstein, J. P. *Prolegomena Ad Litteras Tannaiticas* (Hebrew), 1957.

Falk, Z. W. *Hebrew Law in Biblical Times*. Jerusalem: Wahrmann, 1964.

Fensham, F. C. "The Covenant Idea in the Book of Hosea," *OTWSA* (1964-65): 44.

Fensham, F. C. "The Marriage Metaphor in Hosea for the Covenant Relationship between the Lord and his People," *JNSL* 12 (1984): 71-78.

Foulkes, Francis. *The Epistle of Paul to the Ephesians*. Tyndale New Testament Commentaries. Grand Rapid : Eerdmans, 1983.

Friedman, Mordecai A. "Israel's Response in Hosea 2:17b: 'You Are My Husband,'"*JBL* 99/2 (1980) 199-204.

Galambush, Julie. *Jerusalem in the Book of Ezekiel: The City as Yahweh's Wife*, SBL Dissertation Series130. Atlanta: Scholars Press, 1992.

Geldenhuys, Norvals. *Commentary on the Gospel of Luke*, NICNT. Grand Rapids: Eerdmans, 1951.

Gibson, J. C. L. *Canaanite Myths and Legends*. Edinburgh: T. & T. Clark, 1978.

Ginsberg, H. L. "לקח" in *Yehezjelkaufman Jubille Volume*. ed by M. Haran, Jerusalem: Magness Press, 1960.

Ginsberg, L. *The Legends of the Jews*. Philadelphia: Jewish Publication Society, 1928.

Good, Robert M. *The Sheep of His Pasture: A Study of Hebrew Noun ʿAm(m) and Its Semitic Cognates*, Harvard Semitic Monographs 29. Chico: Scholars Press, 1983.

Gordon, Cyrus H. *Ugaritic Text*. Rome: Pontifical Biblical Institute, 1965

Greenberg, Moshe. *Ezekiel, 1-20*. The Anchor Bible. Garden City: Doubleday, 1990.

Greenberg, Moshe. "Hebrew *segullā*: Akkadian *sikiltu*," *JAOS* 71. (1951): 172-74.

Greengus, S. "The Old Babylonian Marriage Contract" *JAOS* 89.3(1969) : 505-32.

Grelot, P. "The Institution of Marriage: It Evolution in the Old Testament," *Concillium* 55(1970): 39-50.

Haran, M. ed. *Yehezkelkaufman Jubilee Volume.* Jerusalem: Magnes Press, 1960.

Huffmon, H.B. "The Covenant Lawsuit in the Prophets" *JBL* 78 (1959): 285-95.

Hugenberger, G. P. *Marriage as Covenant: A Study of Biblical Law & Ethic Covering Mariage, Developed from the perspective of Malachi.* Leiden: E. J. Brill, 1994.

Hughes, Philip E. *Commentary on the Second Epistle to the Corinthians,* NICNT. Grand Rapids: Eerdmans, 1962.

Hyatt, J. P. *Commentary on Exodus,* The New Century Commentary. London: Oliphants, 1971.

Jeremias, J. J. "νύμφη, νυμφίος" *TDNT,* 1099-1106.

Koehler, L. und W. Baumgartner. *Hebräisches und Aramäisches Lexicons zum Alten Testament.* Leiden: E. J. Brill, 1990.

Kruger, P. A. "The Relationship between Yahweh and Israel as expressed by certain metaphors and similies in the book of Hosea." D. Litt. dissertation, University of Stellenbosh, 1983.

Leeuwen, C. van. *Hosea,* 3 druk. De Prediking van net Oude Testament. Edited by A. van Selms, A.S. van der Woude, and C. van Leeuwen, Nijkerk: G.F. Callenbach, 1984.

Levine, Baruch A. "In Praise of the Isrelite *Mišpaḥah*": Legal Themes in the Book of Ruth," *The Quest of the Kingdom of God: Studies in Honor of George E. Mendenhall*.eds. H.B. Huffmon, et al. Winona Lake: Eisenbrauns, 1983.

Linberg, J. "The Root, *RIB* and Prophetic Lawsuit Speeches," *JBL* 88 (1969): 291-304.

Lincoln, Andrew T. *Ephesians,* World Biblical Commentary 42. Dallas: Word Books, 1990.

Lohfink, N. "Deut. 26:17-19 und die Bundesformel," Zeitschrift für katholische Theologie 91 (1969): 517-53.

Martin, Ralph P. *2 Corinthians,* Word Bible Commentary 40. Waco: Word Books, 1986.

Masterman, E. W. G. "Hygiene and Disease in Palestine," *PEFQS* 50 (1918): 112-19.

McCarthy, D. J. "Three Covenant in Genensis," *CBQ* 26 (1964): 179- 89.

———. *Old Testament Covenant: A Survey of Current Opinion.* Atlanta: John Knox, 1972.

McComskey, T. *Hosea, An Exegetical & Expository Commentary: The Minor Prophets,* ed. Thomas Edward McComskey. Grand Rapids: Baker, 1992.

Nolland, John. *Luke 1-9:20.* Word Biblical Commentary 35A. Dallas: Word, 1989.

Ogden, G. S. "Time and the Verb, היה in O.T. Prose." *VT* 21, 1971.

Owen, D. L. & E. Stone. *Adoption in Old Babylon Nippur and the Archaive of Mannum-mešu-liṣṣur.* Winona Lake: Eisenbrauns, 1991.

Patai, Raphael. *Sex and Family in the Bible and the Middle East.* Garden city: Doubleday, 1959.

Poebel, Amo. "Babylonian Legal and Busienes Documents from the Time of the First Dynasty of Babylon, Chiefly from Nippur (1920)." 6/2 cited in Elizabeth C. Stone and David. L. Owen, *Adoption in Old Babylon Nippur andthe Archive of Manuum-meš-liṣṣur.* Winona Lake: Eisenbrauns, 1991.

Porten, Bezalel and Ada Yardeni, *Textbook of Aramaic Documents From Ancient Egypt,* vol.2: Contract. Jerusalem Hebrew University, 1989.

Prichard, James B. *Ancient Near Eastern Texts Relating to the Old Testament,* ed. Princeton: Princeton University Press, 1969.

Reich N. "Marriage and Divorce in Ancient Egypt: Papyrus Documents Discovered at Thebes by Eckly B. Coxe Jr., Expedition to Egypt," *The Museum Journal.* Philadelphia: University of Pennsylvania, 1924.

Rogers, Robert G. "The Doctrine of Election in the Chronicler's Work and the Dead Sea Scrolls,"Ph.D. Dissertation, Boston University, 1969.

Sarna, Nahum. *Genesis: The JPS Torah Commentary.* Philadelphia: Jewish Publication Society, 1989.

Schiffman, L. H., *Ki Baruch HU: Ancient Near Eastern, Biblical, and Judaic Studies in Honor of Baruch A. Levine.* R. Chazan, W.W. Hallo, and L. Schiffman, eds. Winona Lake: Eisenbrauns, 1999.

Selms, A. Van. *Marriage & Family Life in Ugaritic Literature.* London: Luzac & Co., 1954.

Smend, R. *Die Bundesformel.* Zurich, 1963.

Sohn, Seock-Tae. *The Divine Election of Israel.* Grand Rapids: Eerdmans, 1991.

———. "'I Will Be Your God and You Will Be My People': The Origin and Background of the Covenant Formula." Pages in 355-372 in *Ki Baruch HU: Ancient Near Eastern, Biblical, and Judaic Studies in Honor of Baruch A. Levine.* Edidted by R. Chazan, W.W. Hallo, and L. Schiffman, eds. Winona Lake: Eisenbrauns, 1999.

Speiser, E. A. *Genesis.* Anchor Bible. Garden City Doubleday, 1964.

Stienstra, Nelly. *YHWH is the Husband of His People:Analysis of a Biblical Metaphor with Special Reference to Translatation.* Kampen, The Netherland: Kok Pharos Publishing House, 1993.

Stone, Elizabeth C. and David L. Owen. *Adoption in Old Babylon Nippur and the Archive of Manuum-meš-liṣṣur* . Winona Lake: Eisenbrauns, 1991.

Taylor, John B. *Ezekiel,* Tyndale Old Testament Commentaries 16. Leicester: IVP, 1969.

Thompson, J. A. *The Book of Jeremiah,* NICOT. Grand Rapids: Eerdmans, 1980.

Tregelles, Samuel Predeaux. *Gesenius' Hebrew and Chalde Lexicons to the Old Testament Scripture,* Grand Rapids: Eerdmans, 1952.

Vaux, R. de. *Ancient Israel.* 2 vols. New York: McGrow-Hill, repr.1965.

Weiss, David Halivini. "The Use of hnq in Connection with marriage," *HTR* 57 (1957): 244-48.

Wenham, G. J. *Genesis 1-15,* Word Biblical Commentary, Vol. 1. Waco: Word Books, 1987.

Williamson, H. G. *Ezra, Nehemiah,* Word Biblical Commentary, vol. 6. (Waco: Word Book Publisher,1985), p. 185.

Wiseman, D. J. *The Vassal-Treaties of Esarhadon,* London, 1958.

Wolff, H. W. *Hosea,* Hermenia Series. Philadelphia: Fortress, 1974.

Yaron, R. *The Laws of Eshnunna.* Jerusalem-Leiden: The Magnes Press, E. J. Brill, 1969.

Yaron, R. "Aramaic Marriage Contracts from Elephatine" *JSS* 31(1958): 30-31.

Young, E. J. *The Book of Isaiah,* Vol. 3. Chapters 40-66. A Commentary. Grand Rapids: Eerdmans, 1972.

Zimmerli, Walther. *Ezekiel 1.* Hermeneia. Philadelphia: Fortress, 1979.

Name Index

Albright, W.F., 103n.25
Allen, L., 118n.32
Andersen, F.I., 71n.3,4, 77n.9, 81n.10
Astour, M., 106n.27

Barth, M., 140n.8
Bauer, W., 136n.2
Bright, J., 49n.6, 69n.2, 93n.13
Brown, R.D., 138n.4
Brownlee, W.H., 97n.16, 98n.18, 99n.19
Burrows, M., 10n.9, 16

Campbell, E.F., 59n.11
Chazan, R., 95n.15
Clement, R.E., 8n.4
Cole, A., 32n.30
Cooke, G.A., 97n.16, 100n.20, 119n.33
Cowley, A.P. 17n24, 25n.6
Coxe, E.B. Jr
Craigie, P.C., 40n.6, 42n.9, 91n.12, 93n.14

Davis, T.W.,16n.21
De Vaux, R., 9n.7, 17n.26, 25n.6, 37n.1, 38n.2, 41n.7
DeRoche, M., 14n.20
Durham, J.L., 32n.30

Eissfeldt, O., 107n.28
Epstein, J.N., 10n.11

Falk, Z.W., 34n.32
Fensham, F.C., 71n.3
Foulkes, F., 140n.8
Freedman, D.N., 71n.3,4, 77n.9
Friedman, M.A., 11n.12, 16n.23
Friedman, M.A., 28n.16
Friedman, M.A., 34n.34

Galambush, J., 97n.16
Geldenhuys, 136n.2
Gibson, J.C.L., 7n.3
Ginsberg, L., 10n.11
Ginsberg, L., 49n.6
Good, R.M., 29n.19, 33n.31,32
Gordon, C.H., 11n.14
Greenberg, M., 97n.16, 100n.21,22, 103n.24, 105n26,27, 106n.40, 108n.29
Greengus, S. , 11n.13, 23n.1, 26n.13, 134n.1
Grelot, P., 26n.12

Hallo, W.W., 95n.15
Haran, M., 71n.3
Harris, R., 56n.10
Hoffner, H.A., 98n.17
Huffmon, H.B., 77n.8
Hugenberger, G.P., 23n.2, 26n.11, 34n.34
Hugh, P.E., 138n.5
Hyatt, J.P., 32n.30

Jeremias, J.J., 136n.2,3

Kalluveetil, 27n.14
Klein, E., 32n.29
Kruger, P.A., 71n.4

Leeuween, C. van, 71n.4
Levine, B.A., 10n.10, 95n.15
Linberg, J., 77n.8
Lincoln, A.T., 139n.7
Lohfink, N., 34n.34

Martin, R.P., 138n.6
Masterman, E.W.G., 99n.19
McCarthy, D.J., 46n.3, 77n.8
McComskey, T.E., 72n.4, 73n.6

Nolland, J., 136n.2
Noth, M., 32n.30
Ogden, G.S., 28n.15
Owen, D.L., 25n.5

Patai, R., 21n.32, 100n.22
Poebel, A., 25n.5
Porten, B., 25n.6
Prichard, J.B., 26n.9

Reich, N., 26n.10
Rogers, R.G., 32n.28

Sarna, N. 47n.4

Schiffman, L.H., 95n.15
Selms, A. van, 13n.16
Smend, R., 34n.34
Sohn, S-.T., 1n.1, 8n.5, 20n.30,31, 29n.17, 30n.22,24,25, 34n.34, 44n. 1,2, 50n.7, 55n.8, 71n.3, 95n.15, 143
Speiser, E.A., 19n.29, 19n.29, 38n.2, 39n.4
Stone, E.C., 25n.5

Taylor, J.B., 100n.20, 105n.26, 120n. 36, 127n.37
Thompson, J.A., 49n.6

Ward, J., 68n.1
Weis, D.H., 10n.11
Wenham, G.J., 42n.10, 64n.13
Williamson, G.M., 15n.21
Wiseman, D.J., 73n.5
Wolf, H.W., 18n.27, 81n.10

Yardeni A., 25n.6
Yaron, R., 17n.25, 56n.10, 64n.13, 134n.1

Zimmerli, W., 100n.20, 119n.33, 120n.33,34,35

Scripture Index

The Old Testament

Genesis

2:24	139,140
3:18	90
4:1	19,38
6:4	38
6:18	115
10:15	105
15:16	87
15:18-21	51
16:2	38
17:13	106
17:19	115
18:16-19:38	113
18:19	19,53
19:32,34,35	38
20:12	16
20:3	9, 38
21:3, 22	9,40
22:17	75
22:23	40
24:24,47	40
24:67	15,16,29,39
25:3	40
25:20	29
26:10	38
26:22	77
26:26-34	46
29:18	35,39
29:21	38
29:23	38
29:27	39
29:32	39
30:3	38
31:44-54	46
31:50	26
34:1	40
34:2,7	38
34:4,21	29
35:22	38
38:8,9	38
38:24	40
39:7	38
39:12	38
39:14	38
41:50	40
44:27	40
45:27	12
46:5	12
46:15,20	40
47:11	15
50:13	12

Exodus

1:15-16	43
2:1	71
2:1-10	98
2:23	43
3:8,17	51
5:8	98
6:1	57
6:4	115
6:6-7	44,45
6:7	8,17,31,32,45
6:7-8	13
6:20	6,29
6:23	29
6:25	29
15:13	51
19:4-6	45
19:5	31,47
19:7-25	46
20:5	138
20:14	40
21:2,22	38
21:28	9
22:15	38
23:23	98
23:30	57
24:1	12
24:1-8	46
24:7	46
24:11	46
24:9-11	46
29:45-46	33,51
33:2	57
34:15-17	55
40:34-38	51,52

Leviticus

15:2	106
18:24	112
18:25	90
18:28	90
19:29	90
20:10	40,128
20:23	112
20:26	53
21:4	38
21:7	57

21:14	57	21:13	38	19:2	41
22:13	57	21:21	128	19:22,23	9
22:32	53	22:13-21	39	21:7	21
23:43	15	22:22	9,38	21:13	17
26:1-3,5-6,6-8,10	52	22:23	40	21:19-24	7
26:9	115	22:23,25,27,28	18	21:22	36
26:11,12	51	22:23-27	37		
		22:19,29	57	*Ruth*	
Numbers		22:24	38	1:4	12
2:1	52	22:29	16	1:8	58
2:3-9, 10-17,18-24	52	24:1	9,40,56	1:9	39
9:15-23	52	24:1-3	92	3:1	39
10:33-34	52	24:1,3,4	57	3:9	20,59
15:38	119	24:1-4	64,89	4:5	40
22:6	57	24:2-4	41	4:13	16,29
30:1	39	24:4	9,16,90		
30:9	57	25:5	29	*1 Samuel*	
		26:17-19	28,34	9:12-13	103
		26:18	31	10:3	12
		28:30	18	12:8	15
Deuternomy		28:58-68	58	18:12	12
1:33	52	29:22-29	54,55	18:21	37
4:20	31,45,45	32:10	101	18:27	35
4:34	8,13,43,45,57			25:25-39	12
4:37	50	*Joshuah*		25:39	29,77
5:18	40	2:1	71	25:49	29
7:6	31	6:18	77	25:40	16,29
7:6-7	45	7:16-26	80	25:41	16
7:6-8	45	15:16-17	35	25:43	16,29
7:7	101	24:18	57		
8:18	115			*2 Samuel*	
9:4	101	*Judges*		1:15	39
10:15	50	2:3	57	3:14	18
12:9	51	3:6	29	5:9	29
14:2	31,53	11:1	71	11:4,11	38
20:7	36	14:3	12	11:26	38
20:13-14	7	14:12	39	11:27	12
20:17	9	14:16	39	12:10	16
20:7	18	15:1	38	12:11,24	38
21:11	29	16:1	38	13:11,14	38
21:11-12	36	16:15	39	16:21	38

Scripture Index

16:22	118	23:20	88	1:3	77
20:3	38	25:26	87	4:10	100
				7:13	100

1 Kings

		2 Chronicles		Isaiah	
3:4	103	8:2	15		
4:1	8	10:12	12	2:2	83
8:56	51	25:18	21	2:6-8,20	69
11:1	39	28:18	106	3:14	77
23:7	103			4:1	39
		Ezra		7:3	71

2 Kings

		10:2,10,14,17,18	15	7:7-9	123
4:1	26			8:3	71
4:20	12	Nehemiah		8:19	69
8:35	31	13:27	15	10:5	111
9:24-26	72	13:25	15	11:8	51
10:11	72			37:29	59
14:9	21	Esther		40:11,24	12
14:20	12	1:6	120	41:8	50
15:19	120	2:17	39	41:16	12
16:3	69			41:17	82
16:5-9	69		Job	43:4	50
16:5-20	106	9:3	77	49:8	82
16:7	69			49:14	61
16:8	108,123	Psalms		50:1	57,129
16:13	104	13:4	31	51:13	61
16:15	69	20:1	82	51:17	126
17:1-18	92	35:1	77	51:22	126
17:1-41	70	47:5	50	51:23	120
17:3	120	75:8	126	51:57	120
17:23-24	92	78:55	57	54:1-8	129
17:24,26	15	78:68	50	54:4	116
18:13-16	108	119:154	77	54:4-8	62
20:12-20	123			54:5	129
21:1-9	87	Proverbs		54:6	60,129
21:1-21	105	2:17	61	54:7-8	62,129
21:6	104	6:29	38	54:8	61
21:10-15	86	7:16	100	57:1-10	129
21:11-12	87	30:23	9	57:3	130
23:4	88	31:24	105	57:5	129
23:15	88			57:8	129
23:19	88	Song of Songs		57:13	12

62:1-5	130	13:26	21	16:8	21,59,101
62:4	60,62	14:6	90	16:9-14	101
62:5	9	15:1	57	16:10	101
		16:9	39	16:11-12	101
Jeremiah		16:27	106	16:14	101
1:5	20	18:15	62	16:15-34	97,102
2:1-37	85	19:5	104	16:15-22	102
2:2		21:10	61	16:16	103,104
44,80,85,92,94,101		25:8-11	111	16:17	103
2:2-3	14	25:15-29	126	16:18	103
2:3	85	30:14	61	16:19	103
2:18	124	30:22	94	16:20	103,104
2:21	85	31:31-33	48,64	16:21	103
2:23-25	85	31:31-34	64,94	16:23-29	102,104
2:26-27	93	31:32	12,94	16:26	106
2:27	85	31:33	64	16:27	107
2:29	85	31:34	116	16:28	107
2:31-33	85	33:5	61	16:29	105,107
2:32	61	37:3-5	105	16:30	108
3:1-5	88	37:7	124	16:30-34	107
3:1-10	88	44:11	61	16:32	108
3:1-18	86	44:27	61	16:35-43	108
3:2	90	49:12	126	16:35-59	97,108
3:6	91	49:39	83	16:36	110
3:6-10	91	50:5	65	16:37,39	60
3:6-11	88	52:1-11	105	16:42	110
3:8	56,91,93			16:43	111,114
3:9	93	*Lamentations*		16:44	112
3:12-13	88	3:58	77	16:44-52	111
3:14	14	4:17	124	16:44-59	108,111
3:14-18	88	4:21	126	16:46	112
3:21	61,90			16:47	113
4:11	90	*Ezekiel*		16:50	113
4:30	77	13:36	21	16:52	113
6:30	60	14:8	61	16:53-59	111,113
7:29	90	15:7	61	16:59	114
7:31	104	16:1-5	97	16:60	65
12:12	90,91,92	16:1-63	96	16:60-63	97,114
12:13	91	16:4	98	17:4	105
12:14	91,92	16:6-14	97,99	17:13-17	105
13:25-27	59	16:7	100	22:12	61

Scripture Index

23:1-49	117	23:46-49	127,128	2:8-13	74,77
23:1-4	117,118,126	23:44	38	2:10	79
		23:45	128	2:12	80
23:3	118	27:7	120	2:13	61
23:5	119	34:25	115	2:14-20	79
23:5-8	119	36:33	15	2:15	79
23:5-10	117,118,126	37:26	65,115	2:16	62
		37:27	65	2:16-25	63
23:6	123	38:8	83	2:17	28
23:8	118	38:16	83	2:18	38,81
23:9-10	118	43:9	65	2:19-20	18,27,63
23:10	21,60	44:22	29	2:21-23	74,75,82
23:11	120	54:3	15	2:22-23	72
23:11-13	120			2:23	27
23:11-21	121	*Daniel*		3:1-2	84
23:11-35	117,120,127	3:2	120	3:1-5	68,82
		3:27	120	4:2	90
23:12	122	10:14	83	4:3	90
23:14-18	121			4:6	61
23:17	100	*Hosea*		5:14	12
23:19	121	1:1	68	6:3	20
23:19-21	121	1:1-9	74	8:13	58
23:22	121,124	1:2	15,68	9:1	58
23:22-27	124	1:2-9	70,75,84	9:3	58
23:22-30	121	1:6	12,14	9:10	101
23:22-35	121,124	1:9	56,75	9:15	58
23:24	125	1:10	74,75	11:5	58
23:25	125	1:10-2:2	75	11:8	62
23:26	60	1:11	72,74	11:11	15
23:28	121,124	1:10-2:1	75,82	12:8	105
23:28-35	125	1:10-2:23	68,74,84	12:10	15
23:31	126	1:23	74	13:4	20
23:32	121,124	2:1	27,75	13:4-6	61
23:35	121,124	2:2	41,77	14:9	82
23:36	21, 119	2:2-7	74,76		
23:36-39	126,127	2:3	60	*Joel*	
23:36-49	117,126	2:4	27,56,77	1:18	38
23:38	128	2:5	39	2:27	65
23:40	77	2:5-7	77		
23:42	128	2:6	11	*Amos*	
23:43	128	2:6-7	77	3:2	20

4:2	59	9:15	136	11:1-3	137
9:4	61	19:5	139		
		20:22	126	*Galatians*	
Obadiah		22:2	39	3:7ff	138
1:16	126	25:1-13	137	3:29	138
		26:39	126	6:16	138
Micah					
4:1	83	*Mark*		*Ephesians*	
5:12-14	69	2:19-20	136	1:22-23	139
		10:7	141	5:18-20	139
Habakkuk				5:21	139
2:16	126	*Luke*		5:21-33	
		5:34	136		137,138,139
Zephaniah				5:26	140
1:11	105	*John*		5:27	140
		1:29	135	5:30	140
Haggai		1:36	136	5:31	140
2:23	8	2:1-12	133	5:33	139
		2:4	134,135		
Zechariah		2:10	134	*Philippians*	
14:21	105	3:22-30	133,137		3:3
		3:28-29	135		
Malachi				*Revelation*	
1:2	50	*Romans*		5:7	135
2:14	26	2:29	138	5:9	135
3:17	31	4:9ff	138	6:11	135
				14:10	126
The New Testament		*1 Corinthians*		19:6-9	133
		6:16	141	19:7	135
Matthew					
1:19	37	*2 Corinthians*			

www.ingramcontent.com/pod-product-compliance
Lightning Source LLC
Chambersburg PA
CBHW051938160426
43198CB00013B/2199